Charles Benjamin Norton

The President and his Cabinet, indicating the progress of the government of the United States under the administration of Grover Cleveland

Charles Benjamin Norton

The President and his Cabinet, indicating the progress of the government of the United States under the administration of Grover Cleveland

ISBN/EAN: 9783337184933

Printed in Europe, USA, Canada, Australia, Japan

Cover: Foto ©Suzi / pixelio.de

More available books at www.hansebooks.com

THE PRESIDENT

AND HIS

CABINET

INDICATING THE PROGRESS OF THE GOV-
ERNMENT OF THE UNITED STATES
UNDER THE ADMINISTRA-
TION OF

GROVER CLEVELAND

BY

C. B. NORTON

Editor of the Civil Service Chronicle

"A PUBLIC OFFICE IS A PUBLIC TRUST"

ILLUSTRATED WITH PORTRAITS AND VIEWS

BOSTON
CUPPLES AND HURD, Publishers
1888

Dedicated to
Prosper Bender, M. D., a warm friend and considerate adviser, by
C. B. NORTON.

CONTENTS.

	PAGE
INTRODUCTION	9
CHAPTER I. CLEVELAND'S EARLY DAYS	17
CHAP. II. CLEVELAND AS MAYOR	29
CHAP. III. CLEVELAND AS GOVERNOR	39
CHAP. IV. CLEVELAND AS PRESIDENT	55
CHAP. V. THE STATE DEPARTMENT	103
CHAP. VI. THE TREASURY DEPARTMENT	117
CHAP. VII. THE WAR DEPARTMENT	139
CHAP. VIII. THE NAVY DEPARTMENT	153
CHAP. IX. THE POST OFFICE DEPARTMENT	161
CHAP. X. DEPARTMENT OF THE INTERIOR	171
CHAP. XI. DEPARTMENT OF JUSTICE—DEPARTMENT OF AGRICULTURE—DEPARTMENT OF LABOR—GOVERNMENT PRINTING OFFICE—U. S. CIVIL SERVICE COMMISSION	191
CHAP. XII. ALLEN G. THURMAN	211
CHAP. XIII. OFFICIAL DOCUMENTS	229

LIST OF ILLUSTRATIONS.

GROVER CLEVELAND, President,	*Frontispiece*
THE CITY HALL, Buffalo, N. Y.,	29
THE STATE HOUSE, Albany, N. Y.,	39
THE EXECUTIVE MANSION, Washington, D. C.,	55
T. F. BAYARD, Secretary of State,	103
C. S. FAIRCHILD, Secretary of the Treasury,	117
WM. C. ENDICOTT, Secretary of War,	139
W. C. WHITNEY, Secretary of the Navy,	153
DON M. DICKINSON, Postmaster-General,	161
WM. F. VILAS, Secretary of the Interior,	171
A. H. GARLAND, Attorney-General,	191
ALLEN G. THURMAN, candidate for Vice-President,	211
RESIDENCE OF ALLEN G. THURMAN, Columbus, O.	217
THE CAPITOL, Washington, D. C.,	229

WORDS OF ACKNOWLEDGMENT.

In the preparation of this work, the writer has had recourse to the biographies of Mr. Cleveland published in 1884, written by Gen. La Fevre, Deshler Welch, Thomas W. Handford, and others, to all of whom he desires to express his obligations; also specially to the heads of departments, chief clerks, and other officers of the Administration, for their uniform courtesy and kindness. The admirable portraits of the Cabinet officers are from photographs by C. M. Bell; the one of the President, by Merritt & Van Wagner, — all used by permission, for which thanks are now returned.

C. B. N.

INTRODUCTION.

THERE can be no doubt that the present condition of this country is a very satisfactory one to the majority of its citizens. That this is largely due to the existence of an honest and thorough business administration, and the enforcement of a statesmanlike foreign and domestic policy, are facts that hardly any but the most bigoted partisan will challenge.

It is equally true that Grover Cleveland has given more time and closer supervision to the duties of his office, and administered the affairs of the country more safely, economically, and judiciously, than any of his predecessors in time of peace. There is no department of the government with the work of which he is not fully acquainted, and all the officers of the government testify to his minute and conscientious inquiry into all matters submitted to him. And yet he finds time to receive all callers at the White House, which he does with that simple, straightforward, and hearty manner which has won him the affection and esteem of all who have come in contact with him; even his political opponents do not leave his presence without experiencing the greatest respect for their host.

We think that we may dare to assert that no President, since the foundation of the government, has shown greater wisdom in the safe guarding of the institutions of the country, given more encouragement and judicious protection to our industries, inaugurated better or sounder policies, enacted more desirable laws, advocated a more beneficial revision of the tariff system, or administered the affairs of the country with greater integrity or stricter economy than Grover Cleveland.

In brief, Grover Cleveland has been the highest exponent of the great principles of Democracy and economical government. His past is a pledge for the future, and, if he be given an opportunity to carry out the reforms he advocates with such characteristic courage and patriotism, including the revision of the present tariff laws and the reduction of the national taxation, a greater era of peace, prosperity, and happiness than ever known in our annals is before us.

With the view of placing before our fellow-citizens the practical and beneficial results of the Cleveland *régime*, and to comply with innumerable requests for more information concerning the past and present of our chief of state, this work has been prepared.

We shall devote some space to a biographical sketch of our illustrious countryman, and give besides many interesting facts regarding the operation of the different departments which he controls, and for which he is responsible to the country.

It will be shown that under

THE STATE DEPARTMENT

our foreign relations have steadily and satisfactorily improved, that our consular service was never so effective, that the valuable weekly and monthly reports supplied by the consuls are already yielding important results, such as the adoption of the suggestions therein contained by our inventors and manufacturers, with all the benefits which that implies.

The effect of the wise and safe financial policy of

THE TREASURY DEPARTMENT

will be fully established. Under the able supervision of the secretary, the work of the department has been greatly simplified and rendered more practicable. Through the adoption and enforcement of the rules of merit service, there has been secured a great economy in the general management of the department, while the assurance of permanence in office during good behavior has resulted in the best and most reliable work being obtained.

We will show that

THE WAR DEPARTMENT

has not by any means been idle. The appropriations of Congress have been expended advantageously and with excellent discrimination, and to-day the guns and projectiles manufactured in this country compare favorably with those of Europe.

Through the systematic work of

THE NAVY DEPARTMENT,

a navy is being rapidly created which will be a credit to the United States. Had not the secretary been hampered by the condition of things in the department when he entered the office, more would have been accomplished; but the work achieved thus far inspires hope and confidence in the mind of all patriotic Americans.

A pronounced and decided advance has been made in

THE INTERIOR DEPARTMENT,

particularly in the general land office, through which agency there have been redeemed, from the hands of jobbers and speculators, millions of acres that are now restored to the public domain, and will in the course of time be homes for coming generations. In the Indian Bureau, where good management and economy are the order of the day, and in the Bureau of Pensions, Patents, and Education, etc., an equally gratifying state of things exists.

THE POST-OFFICE DEPARTMENT

presents a remarkable increase in the facilities for delivering mails, a great economy in the general management of the department, a reduction in the rates of postage, and more rapid and certain delivery of all mail matter.

There has also been a great and marked improvement in the very important work of

THE DEPARTMENT OF JUSTICE,

under the able and experienced management of the attorney-general. There has been a clearing-off of the accumulated work on hand, and special attention is being paid to the important matter of pardons, every case of which receives, in addition, the careful consideration of the President himself.

The farmers of our land have reason to feel grateful for the work of

THE DEPARTMENT OF AGRICULTURE,

which has done so much for the great practical interests of the country.

The introduction of new opportunities for the increase of our agricultural resources will be fully shown in the account of this department.

Under its zealous, capable, and experienced chief,

THE DEPARTMENT OF LABOR

is rendering incalculable benefit to this nation at large. This is additional evidence that no point is overlooked, under the present administration, that will benefit our people.

THE CIVIL SERVICE COMMISSION

is engaged in one of the most difficult tasks ever attempted in connection with the administration of any government. The patience and perseverance of the commissioners deserve all praise, and the result of their labors will convince our readers of the really wonderful progress already secured, cavillers notwithstanding.

With such a record as the above, is it not reasonable to believe that the independent thinker and non-partisan voter will unite with the Democratic party to secure a perpetuation of so satisfactory a condition of things? With Grover Cleveland at the helm of the ship of state, during the next four years, we may look forward to broad, liberal, and enlightened tariff reform measures, to comprehensive and successful financial policies, and to marked progress and efficiency in the merit service of the United States.

No man stands higher to-day in the peerage of public esteem and affection than Grover Cleveland,

and all true patriots must earnestly desire to see him for another term occupy the exalted position of the ruler of the destinies of the greatest nation on the face of the earth, in which he now figures so creditably and honorably.

THE PRESIDENT AND HIS CABINET.

CHAPTER I.

CLEVELAND'S EARLY DAYS.

THAT the President of the United States occupies the highest position among the rulers of the world cannot be denied. When we take into consideration the enormous extent of territory, the large and intelligent population, and the varied nationalities represented in this country, this fact must be admitted. While the Queen of England and Empress of India and the Czar of Russia govern millions who neither know nor care as to the personality of their ruler, the sixty millions of our citizens are all interested to know of Grover Cleveland. For that reason a sketch of his ancestry and early life is here presented, with the view of supplying information from authentic sources and in a popular form for the use of the people.

In 1635, Moses Cleveland came to America from Ipswich, Suffolk County, in England; he died in Woburn, Mass., January 9, 1701, and in the old graveyard of that town are still standing headstones of English slate which indicate the resting-place of Aaron Cleveland, the second son of Moses, and the great-grandfather of the President. He was one of the early opponents of slavery, and will long be remembered as having introduced a bill in the Legislature of the State of Connecticut for its abolition. He studied divinity and became a Congregational minister, and died in New Haven, 1815. William, the second son of Aaron Cleveland, and the grandfather of the President, was a practical silversmith at Beacon Hill, near Norwich, Conn.; he retired from business and moved to New York State, dying at Black Rock, in 1857.

Richard F. Cleveland, the second son of William, and father of the President, was born in Norwich, Conn., 1804. He graduated at Yale College in 1824, locating in Baltimore as a teacher, and while engaged in his duties pursued his studies for the ministry. In 1828, he was ordained a Presbyterian minister in Windham, near Norwich. The following year he married the daughter of Abner Neal of Baltimore, and later on settled at Caldwell, N. J. Thence he removed to Fayetteville, N. Y., in 1841, and in 1847 he was appointed secretary of the Home Missionary Society. Six years afterwards he was installed at Holland Patent, where he died October 1, 1853, in his fiftieth year. Mrs. Cleveland, mother of the President, died in the same place, July 19, 1882.

Grover Cleveland was born in Caldwell, N. J., March 18, 1837. The house, a small, unpretending cottage, still remains, and it has attracted many visitors to Caldwell, from its connection with the childhood of the President. The father, grandfather, and great-grandfather of the President were natives of Connecticut.

When Grover Cleveland was five years of age, his father became pastor of a church in Fayetteville, N. Y., and there the son attended school and was for a time a clerk in a country store, thus growing up among the people as one of themselves. In the character of the President there is evidence of the advantages secured by an intermingling of the old Puritan stock with that of the Cavaliers of Maryland. While the family resided in Clinton, the seat of Hamilton College, he continued his preparations for entering college. His father's health not being satisfactory, another removal was made to Holland Patent, where the sudden decease of the elder Cleveland changed the future life of the son. William, an elder brother, occupied a responsible position as instructor in the Institution for the Blind in New York City, and, although but sixteen years of age, Grover also obtained employment, through the influence of Augustus Schell, formerly collector of that port. In this position the young man did his duty with faithfulness, and it is doubtless due to this experience with the blind that the President possesses a patience and perseverance for which he has universal credit. After some time spent in New York, he determined to go West; but an interview with his uncle, Lewis F. Allen, changed his plans, and, through the suggestions and advice of Mr. Allen, he located in Buffalo, entering the law office of Rogers, Bowen & Rogers, as an office boy, upon a salary of four dollars a week, and walking from his uncle's house, two miles from the office, in all weathers. It was a position which, in itself, required detail, and Grover Cleveland soon indicated his natural tendency to system and order, an experience which has largely facilitated him in the control and management of the enormous amount of business which now falls to him to supervise and complete. He was a hard worker, studied his profession carefully in all his spare time, and progressed so rapidly as to attract the attention of his employers. After four years' hard work he became managing clerk.

It is stated by those who knew Grover Cleveland at this period of his life that he won success by his industry, courage, and honesty. He was thorough in all he undertook, and, once his convictions were formed upon what he believed to be reliable data, nothing could change them. In 1859, when he was in his twenty-second year, he completed his legal studies, passed the necessary examinations, and was admitted to the bar. It was at this period in his life that he adopted a rule to complete every day's work so that it would not have to be done again, and the late hours kept by the President at his desk in the executive mansion bear testimony to the value of a plan which he still adheres to.

During his connection with the bar at Buffalo, he was intrusted with some important cases, which were so successfully conducted that he was at once recognized as a rising man in his profession. On January 1, 1863, Grover Cleveland was appointed assistant district attorney of Erie County. This position was a close test of his abilities, and the universally expressed opinion of all who knew him was that in that office he did an amount of work seldom accomplished. He still maintained his resolution to complete the day's duties, and often, when it became necessary, could be found busy till an early hour in the morning. During his occupation of the office, nearly the entire range of duties fell upon his shoulders; it was just the training he needed, and he went into it with all the zeal of youthful aspirations. He was in attendance at all the grand jury meetings during his three-years term of office, and presented in full a large majority of the cases. However, before the three years had elapsed, the people of Buffalo were so well satisfied with the colors of Grover Cleveland that he was unanimously nominated for district attorney by the Democrats of Buffalo, at the age of twenty-nine, but was beaten by his intimate personal friend, Lyman K. Bass, with whom he afterwards formed a law partnership — in 1866. Mr. Cleveland formed a partnership with the late mayor of Buffalo, I. V. Vanderpoel, which lasted till 1869, when he joined the firm of Laning, Cleveland & Folsom. In 1870 the friends of Grover Cleveland suggested his name as candidate for the office of sheriff, and, without any effort on his part, he received the unanimous vote of the Democratic party, and was elected for three years. The office of sheriff is the most important executive office in the county, under the system in the State of New York. The duties of this position were filled by Mr. Cleveland with the same attention and business-like fidelity that he had always shown in such positions as he had held either in public or private life. In this, the first important executive position which he had filled, he did justice to himself and to those whose confidence he had secured, and by whom he was elected. While holding this important office, Grover Cleveland's habits were simple and unassuming, the fees of the sheriff's office were sufficiently large to admit of saving some money, and, had he been ambitious in that direction, he could have been a rich man.

At the expiration of his official term as sheriff, in 1873, he became a member of the firm of Messrs. Bass, Cleveland, and Bissell, with Lyman K. Bass and Wilson S. Bissell as associates. This was a strong and popular firm, and commanded a large and lucrative practice. In 1881 a new firm was formed, Mr. George J. Sicard being admitted as a partner under the firm name of Cleveland, Bissell & Sicard, which still exists. It was in this position that Mr. Cleveland secured a permanent reputation in that section of the State of New York for legal acumen and intellectual honesty. His management of cases was distinguished by sound views, direct simple logic, and a thorough mastery of all their intricacies, which secured for him the respect of his own profession and the admiration of the public. These qualities, combined with the fidelity and independence of his official action, naturally secured for him the general respect and esteem of his fellow-citizens. The best evidence of this are the numerous statements that have appeared in type, voluntarily contributed by citizens of western New York.

Judge George W. Clinton, the son of Governor De Witt Clinton, and vice-chancellor of the University of New York, chief judge of the Superior Court, before whom Grover Cleveland frequently appeared, says of him: "As a lawyer he was known both as a counsellor and an advocate, and he often appeared before a jury. In his jury addresses he never fired over the heads of the jury in rhetorical eloquence. He addressed himself to them directly, as an honest, sensible man speaking to his fellows, and he won his verdicts by his close and full argument, and his thorough knowledge of all the evidence in the case. He was strictly honorable, and never endeavored to take petty advantages of the opposing counsel or of the jury. So keen was his sense of honor and justice that it would have gone against the grain of his character to have tried to mislead a jury if justice was opposed to him. I certainly never knew him to make the effort. When he began practice his reputation as a lawyer was respectable. It rose gradually among the profession until at the time he became mayor he can truthfully be said to have been eminent at the bar of Erie County."

Mr. Milburn, a well known lawyer of Buffalo, states as follows in reference to Mr. Cleveland: "He is a fine lawyer. He is incapable of wilful wrong, and nothing on earth could sweep him from his conviction of duty. That he is thoroughly honest cannot be questioned, and he has always been regarded as an able and safe man in every relation of life." Mr. James N. Matthews, editor of the leading *Republican* paper in Buffalo, utters the same sentiments: "I know of no Democrat better equipped for the position for which he has been named than Grover Cleveland. He is an able, honest, and incorruptible man. He is self-reliant, and has excellent judgment. He has long stood in the front rank with the very leaders of thought and action in this part of New York." At this time, 1881, there was a strong revolt against the management of the municipal affairs of the city of Buffalo, and in this condition of affairs the old party lines were to a certain extent disorganized. It had been badly ruled by a combination of Republican managers, and many voters took exceptions to an extension of this fraud and mismanagement. The city was ring-ridden, its revenues were stolen or wasted, and no mayor had been found, for many years, who possessed the courage and ability to attack these abuses. To secure such a mayor was no easy task. There were many who were profuse in their promises, but such pledges had been so often broken that the citizens intended that no one should be promoted to the place who could not give good security by means of an unsullied reputation and a good record. At this time the Democratic party was the party of reform, and Grover Cleveland participated in a movement which he believed to be just and right. As sheriff of Erie County, he secured administrative reform, and the respect he received from his fellow-citizens on retiring from that office is the best testimony to his success. A candidate for mayor was needed whose honesty should be unimpeachable, and whose courage would enable him to stem the torrent of political corruption. The people turned to Grover Cleveland as the man for the occasion. At first he declined; he did not desire the nomination, but suggested the names of several prominent Democratic citizens as far more available than himself for the position. However, the strong pressure brought to bear by some of the best men in Buffalo at last convinced him of the importance of his acceptance of the nomination, and he did so. There can be no question but that in this case the office sought the man. At the Buffalo Democratic City Convention in 1881, in accepting the nomination, Grover Cleveland placed himself upon a platform which appeals to-day with equal force to the entire voting population of these United States. He said, "Gentlemen of the Convention, I am informed that you have bestowed upon me the nomination for the office of mayor. It certainly is a great honor to be thought fit to be the chief officer of a great and prosperous city like ours, having such important and varied interests. I hoped that your choice might fall upon some other and more worthy member of the city Democracy, for personal and private considerations have made the question of acceptance on my part a difficult one. But because I am a Democrat and because I think no one has a right at this time of all others to consult his own inclinations as against the call of his party and fellow-citizens, and hoping that I may be of use to you in your efforts to inaugurate a better rule in municipal affairs, I accept the nomination tendered to me. I believe much can be done to relieve our citizens from their present load of taxation, and that a more rigid scrutiny of all public expenditures will result in a great saving to the community. I also believe that some extravagances in our city government may be corrected without injury to the public service. There is, or there should be, no reason why the affairs of our city should not be managed with the same care and the same economy as private interests. And when we consider that public officials are the trustees of the people, and hold their places and exercise their powers for the benefit of the people, there should be no higher inducement to a faithful and honest discharge of public duty.

"These are very old truths; but I cannot forbear to speak in this strain to-day, because I believe the time has come when the people loudly demand that these principles shall be sincerely, and without mental reservation, adopted as a rule of conduct. And I am assured that the result of the campaign upon which we enter to-day will demonstrate that the citizens of Buffalo will not tolerate the man or the party who has been unfaithful to public trusts. I say these things to a convention of Democrats, because I know that the grand old party is honest, and they cannot be unwelcome to you. Let us, then, in all sincerity, promise the people an improvement in our municipal affairs, and, if the opportunity is offered to us, as it surely will be, let us faithfully keep that promise. By this means, and by this means alone, can our success rest upon a firm foundation, and our party ascendancy be permanently assured. Our opponents will wage a bitter and determined warfare; but, with united and hearty effort, we shall achieve a victory for our entire ticket. And at this day, and with my record before you, I trust it is unnecessary for me to pledge to you my most earnest endeavors to bring about this result; and, if elected to the position for which you have nominated me, I shall do my whole duty to the party, but none the less, I hope, to the citizens of Buffalo."

The result of such an address as this may easily be imagined. Speaking, as it did, to the sound, practical common-sense of those who listened to it, the effect was like magic. Every independent reform voter felt that his own views would be carried out to the best interests of the city of Buffalo. The truth of every word uttered by Grover Cleveland was at once admitted, and, up to this time, not even his bitterest foe has dared to question the perfect honesty of his opinions. No better evidence of the non-partisan feeling in Buffalo can be produced than the following, from a leading editorial in the Buffalo *Express*, a well known and prominent *Republican* paper, — "The Man for Mayor." "Circumstances seem at last to have brought to the front the right man for this great place, and it only remains to be seen whether the people will have wisdom enough to put him in it. We know Grover Cleveland. Nearly all of his fellow-citizens are aware of his distinguished abilities and reputation as a lawyer, of his great personal worth, of his unswerving uprightness, and of his high moral courage. But *we* know something more than all this. It has happened to us to have personal experience of that sleepless vigilance, that tireless devotion, that singular penetration, and that broad good judgment which Mr. Cleveland has always displayed in the interest of his clients, and from which so many have reaped the reward of a righteous verdict. If he is mayor, the city will be to him as his client,— as a client standing more sorely in need of all his best endeavors than any one he ever served before,— and woe would be to the man that should attempt to rob or otherwise wrong her." What better statement can be put before the people of the United States than the evidence that this honesty of purpose, this decision of character, this care for the public welfare, has consistently been the aim of Grover Cleveland, as mayor of Buffalo, Governor of the Empire State, and President of the United States!

THE CITY HALL, BUFFALO, N.Y.

CHAPTER II.

GROVER CLEVELAND AS MAYOR.

Reform was the watchword which elected Mr. Cleveland mayor of the city of Buffalo. This election was in itself an almost unparalleled triumph, demonstrating the confidence which the people had in his integrity, and his special fitness to carry out the needed reforms in the city government, and it settled the issue of the hour, that it was possible to secure by a popular election that kind of integrity and sagacity that would administer the people's affairs with the honesty and discretion that was necessary to good government. Upon his inauguration as mayor, he took occasion immediately to reiterate the principles of action which he had affirmed in his speech accepting the nomination. So soon as he was elected, he devoted his time to a careful study of the departments of the city government, and he made it clear, too, that in all of these and in all subordinate positions he was firmly determined that the principles he had laid down for himself should be implicitly obeyed by others. In his inaugural message to the common council of Buffalo, on January 2, 1882, he set forth these principles in the following vigorous and direct language:—

To the Honorable the Common Council of the City of Buffalo.

In presenting to you my first official communication, I am by no means unmindful of the fact that I address a body many of the members of which have had quite a large experience in municipal affairs, and which is directly charged, more than any other instrumentality, with the management of the government of the city, and the protection of the interest of all the people within its limits. This condition of things creates grave responsibilities, which I have no doubt you fully appreciate. It may not be amiss, however, to remind you that our fellow-citizens, just at this time, are particularly watchful of those in whose hands they have placed the administration of the city government, and demand of them the most watchful care and conscientious economy. We hold the money of the people in our hands, to be used for their purposes, and to further their interests as members of the municipality; and it is quite apparent that, when any part of the funds which the taxpayers have thus intrusted us are diverted to other purposes, or when by design or neglect we allow a greater sum to be applied to any municipal purpose than is necessary, we have to that extent violated our duty. There surely is no difference in his duties and obligations whether a person is intrusted with the money of one man or many. And yet it sometimes appears as though the office-holder assumes that a different rule of fidelity prevails between him and the taxpayer than that which should regulate his conduct when as an individual he holds the money of his neighbor.

It seems to me that a successful and faithful administration of the government of our city may be accomplished by constantly bearing in mind that we are the trustees and agents of our fellow-citizens, holding their funds in sacred trust, to be expended for their benefit; that we should at all times be prepared to render an honest account of them, touching the manner of their expenditure, and that the affairs of the city should be conducted, as far as possible, upon the same principles as a good business man manages his private concerns. And I perhaps should do no less then than to assure your honorable body that, so far as it is in my power, I shall be glad to coöperate with you in securing the faithful performance of official duty in every department of the city government.

It was at the time when Grover Cleveland was elected mayor of Buffalo that the subject of civil service reform commenced to attract serious attention, and it can be stated with truth that he was one of the first to give it practical use. In his inaugural message, referring to the office of city auditor, he said, — "It seems to me that the duties which should be performed by this officer have been entirely misapprehended. I understand that it has been supposed that he does all that is required of him when he tests the correctness of the extensions and footings of an account presented to him, copies the same in a book, and audits the same as charged, if the extensions and footings are found correct. This work is certainly not difficult, and might well be done by a lad but slightly acquainted with figures. The charter requires that this officer 'shall examine and report upon all unliquidated claims against the city, before the same shall be audited by the common council.' Is it not very plain that the examination of a claim means something more than the footing of the account by which that claim is represented? And is it not equally plain that the report provided for includes more than the approval of all accounts which *on their face* appear correct? There is no question but that he should inquire into the *merits* of the claims presented to him, and he should be fitted to do so by a familiarity with the value of the articles and services embodied in the accounts. In this way, he may protect the interest of the city; otherwise, his services are worse than useless, so far as his action is relied upon." As regards the duties of officials, Mayor Cleveland was equally strong and definite. "I am utterly unable to discover any valid reason why the city offices should be closed, and the employés released from their duties, at the early hour in the day which seems now to be regarded as the limit of a day's work. I am sure no man would think an active private business was well attended to if he and all his employés ceased work at four o'clock in the afternoon. The salaries paid by the city, to its officers and their employés, entitle it to a fair day's work. Besides, these offices are for the transaction of public business, and the convenience of all our citizens should be consulted in respect to the time during which they should remain open.

"I suggest the passage of an ordinance prescribing such hours for the opening and closing of the city offices as shall subserve the public convenience. It would be very desirable if some means could be devised to stop the practice, so prevalent among our city employés, of selling or assigning in advance their claims against the city for services to be rendered. The ruinous discounts charged and allowed greatly diminish the reward of their labors. In many cases, habits of improvidence and carelessness are engendered, and in all cases this hawking and trafficking in claims against the city presents a humiliating spectacle. In conclusion, I desire to disclaim any dictation as to the performance of your duties. I recognize fully the fact that with you rests the responsibility of all legislation which touches the prosperity of the city and the correction of abuses. I do not arrogate to myself any great familiarity with municipal affairs, nor any superior knowledge of the city's needs. I speak to you not only as the chief executive officer of the city, but as a citizen proud of its progress and commanding position. In this spirit the suggestions contained herein are made. If you deem them worthy of consideration, I shall still be anxious to aid the adoption and enforcement of any measures which you may inaugurate looking to the advancement of the interests of the city and the welfare of its inhabitants."

These words afforded ample evidence to the fellow-citizens of Grover Cleveland that in his election they had secured the purification of the municipal government, the hope of which had contributed so much to the great majority by which the election had been carried. His views regarding the freedom of the citizens are best understood from the remarks made at a mass meeting of Irish-American citizens, at which Mayor Cleveland presided. He spoke as follows: "Fellow-Citizens: This is the formal mode of address on occasions of this kind, but I think we seldom realize fully its meaning, or how valuable a thing it is to be a citizen. From the earliest civilization, to be a citizen has been to be a free man, endowed with certain privileges and advantages, and entitled to the full protection of the state. The defence and protection of the personal rights of its citizens has always been the paramount and most important duty of a free, enlightened government.

"And perhaps no government has this sacred trust more in its keeping than this, the best and freest of them all, for here the people who are to be protected are the source of those powers which they delegate upon the express compact that the citizens shall be protected. For this purpose we choose those who, for the time being, shall manage the machinery which we have set up for our defence and safety. And this protection adheres to us in all lands and places as an incident of citizenship. Let but the weight of a sacrilegious hand be put upon this sacred thing, and a great strong government springs to its feet to avenge the wrong. Thus it is that the native-born American citizen enjoys his birthrights. But when, in the westward march of empire, this nation was founded and took root, we beckoned to the old world and invited hither its immigration, and provided a mode by which those who sought a home among us might become our fellow-citizens. They came by thousands and hundreds of thousands; they came and

> Hewed the dark old woods away,
> And gave the virgin fields to day.

They came with strong sinews and brawny arms to aid in the growth and progress of a new country; they came and upon our altars laid their fealty and submission; they came to our temples of justice, and under the solemnity of an oath renounced all allegiance to every other state, potentate, and sovereignty, and surrendered to us all the duty pertaining to such allegiance. We have accepted their fealty, and invited them to surrender the protection of their native land.

"And what should we give them in return? Manifestly, good faith and every dictate of honor demand that we give them the same liberty and protection here and elsewhere which we vouchsafe to our native-born citizens. And that this has been accorded to them is the crowning glory of American institutions. It needed not the statute which is now the law of the land, declaring that 'all naturalized citizens while in foreign lands are entitled to and shall receive from this government the same protection of person and property which is accorded to native-born citizens,' to voice the policy of our nation. In all lands where the semblance of liberty is preserved, the right of a person arrested to a speedy accusation and trial is or ought to be a fundamental law, as it is a rule of civilization. At any rate, we hold it to be so, and this is one of the rights which we undertake to guarantee to any native-born or naturalized citizen of ours, whether he be imprisoned by order of the Czar of Russia or under the pretext of a law administered for the benefit of the landed aristocracy of England. We do not claim to make laws for other countries, but we do insist that, whatsoever these laws may be, they shall, in the interests of human freedom and the rights of mankind, so far as they involve the liberty of our citizens, be speedily administered. We have a right to say, and do say, that mere suspicion, without examination or trial, is not sufficient to justify the long imprisonment of a citizen of America. Other nations may permit their citizens to be thus imprisoned. Ours will not. And this, in effect, has been solemnly declared by statute. We have met here to-night to consider this subject, and to inquire into the cause and the reasons and the justice of the imprisonment of certain of our fellow-citizens now held in British prisons without the semblance of a trial or legal examination. Our law declares that the government shall act in such cases. But the people are the creators of the government. The undaunted apostle of the Christian religion, imprisoned and persecuted, appealing centuries ago to the Roman law and the rights of Roman citizenship, boldly demanded, ' Is it lawful for you to secure a man that is a Roman and uncondemned?' So, too, might we ask, appealing to the law of our land and the laws of civilization, ' Is it lawful that these, our fellows, be imprisoned, who are American citizens and uncondemned?' I deem it an honor to be called upon to preside at such a meeting, and I thank you for it." This frank, honest, and manly statement as to the rights of our foreign-born citizens in other lands secured for Mr. Cleveland the unswerving attachment of our Irish fellow-citizens, who have ever remained his warm friends.

Grover Cleveland has secured for himself the honorable titles of Veto Mayor, Veto Governor, and Veto President; honorable because that in every instance the reasons for his vetoes were of such a character as to at once impress the good sound common-sense of the country that they were based on good grounds, and were the only means by which fraud and corruption could be stamped out forever. While the mayor may have made some enemies among those whose plans for extravagance were interrupted, and others whose interests were affected, yet it is a most gratifying fact that the large mass of his fellow-citizens were heartily with him in his efforts to do the best in his power for the good of the city, without regard to friend or foe.

There were also many instances where expenditures of money, right enough in themselves, were yet in direct violation of the city charter or the constitution. The legal and acutely honest mind of the mayor at once noted these objections, and never hesitated to apply the veto when necessary. A very interesting case, attracting much attention, was in connection with an appropriation which had passed the city council, for the benefit of a benevolent institution. The mayor, in his veto message, said:—

> I have taxed my ingenuity to discover a way to consistently approve of this resolution, but have been unable to do so. It seems to me that it is not only obnoxious to the provisions of the constitution above quoted, but that it also violates that section of the charter of the city which makes it a misdemeanor to appropriate money raised for one purpose to any other object. Under this section, I think, money raised "for the celebration of the Fourth of July and the reception of distinguished persons" *cannot* be devoted to the observance of Decoration Day. I deem the object of this appropriation a most worthy one. The efforts of our veteran soldiers to keep alive the memory of their fallen comrades certainly deserve the aid and encouragement of their fellow-citizens. We should all, I think, feel it a duty and a privilege to contribute to the funds necessary to carry out such a purpose, and I should be much disappointed if an appeal to our citizens for voluntary subscriptions for this patriotic object should be in vain. . . . I cannot rid myself of the idea that this city government, in its relation to the taxpayers, is a business establishment, and that it is placed in our hands to be conducted on business principles. This theory does not admit of our donating the public funds in the manner contemplated by the action of your honorable body. I deem it my duty, therefore, to return both the resolutions referred to without my approval.
>
> GROVER CLEVELAND.

In this connection it may be mentioned that the mayor put his hand in his pocket, and made a liberal subscription towards the expenses of Decoration Day. As may well have been expected, his administration of the government of the city of Buffalo upon business principles was a pronounced success. A very large amount of money was saved to the voters under his management, and the city improved in every direction. The natural result of this successful reform movement on the part of Grover Cleveland was to turn the attention of the people of the Empire State to the value of his services, and in the line of promotion he was selected as the proper candidate for the position of Governor of the State of New York, and was elected by nearly two hundred thousand majority.

THE CAPITOL, ALBANY, N.Y.

CHAPTER III.

GROVER CLEVELAND AS GOVERNOR.

The best evidence as to the fitness of Grover Cleveland for the office of Governor of the Empire State is the following panegyric of that able and well known *Republican* journal The Buffalo *Express:*

> The most promising and prominent of the possible candidates for Governor of New York, on the Democratic side, is a man who, this time last year, had hardly been thought of as a candidate for mayor of Buffalo. It was with the utmost difficulty that he could be persuaded to accept that nomination. He didn't want the office. Only at a great sacrifice of professional income and comfort could he discharge its duties. An election could not gratify his ambition, if he had any, because, many years before, he had filled a more lucrative public position, and one that was more desirable to any man who cared to be an influential practical politician. He had no such desire. But, after much importunity, with extreme genuine reluctance, he at length yielded his own preference and allowed his friends to nominate him. He was elected by a majority of three thousand five hundred and thirty, the largest majority ever given to any candidate for that office, though running on the Democratic ticket, and in a city which at the same time gave a majority of one thousand six hundred and twenty-four for the Republican State ticket, and his administration of the office has fully justified the partiality of the friends who insisted upon nominating him, and vindicated the good judgment of the people who so powerfully insisted upon electing him. It is not too much to say that in the first half of his first year he has almost revolutionized our municipal govern-

ment. With no more power then his predecessors had, he has inaugurated reforms heretofore only hoped for, and corrected abuses which had become almost venerable. Accounts against the city are now thoroughly audited, since he pointed out what is required of an officer whose duty it is to audit. The wholesome rule of competition has been adopted for important work hitherto given out in the form of political patronage. So far as one man can, he sees to it that the city gets the full value of its money. He knows his power and is not afraid to use it. He has conquered the most corrupt combination ever formed in the council. His veto messages have become municipal classics. Knowing his duty, he has faithfully performed it,— with what benefit to the public, can hardly be overestimated.

Statements of this stamp in prominent *Republican* journals had great weight in the approaching election for Governor, and it is not at all surprising that Grover Cleveland received a majority of 192,854, being nearly four times the majority received by either Grant for President in 1872, or Tilden for Governor in 1874. The New York *Sun*, edited by Charles A. Dana, heartily endorsed the nomination of Cleveland, and editorially said, "Grover Cleveland, now mayor of Buffalo and the Democratic candidate for Governor of New York, *is a man worthy of the highest public confidence.* No one can study the record of his career since he has held office in Buffalo, without being convinced that he possesses those highest qualities of a public man, sound principles of administrative duty, luminous intelligence, and courage to do what is right no matter who may be pleased or displeased thereby. . . . No matter what political faith a man now prefer to be called, no one can consider such principles and sentiments as those declared by Mr. Cleveland without feeling that such a public officer is worthy of the confidence and support of the whole people, and that the interests of the Empire State will be entirely safe in his hands."

The best evidence of the sterling honesty and ability of Mr. Cleveland, of his determination to act justly, without regard to party, and his special attention to great public trust, may be found in his letter accepting the nomination, which we give herewith in full, and beg to call the special attention of all of our readers to its high tone, dignified utterances, and yet its perfect simplicity and easily understood statements, making it a primer for the people.

MR. CLEVELAND'S LETTER.

BUFFALO, October 7, 1882.

HON. THOMAS C. E. ECCLESINE, Chairman, etc. :

Dear Sir, I beg to acknowledge the receipt of your letter, informing me of my nomination for Governor by the Democratic State convention, lately held at the city of Syracuse.

I accept the nomination thus tendered to me, and trust that, while I am gratefully sensible of the honor conferred, I am also properly impressed with the responsibilities which it invites.

The platform of principles adopted by the convention meets with my hearty approval. The doctrines therein enunciated are so distinctly and explicitly stated that their amplification seems scarcely necessary. If elected to the office for which I have been nominated, I shall endeavor to impress them upon my administration and make them the policy of the State.

Our citizens for the most part attach themselves to one or the other of the great political parties ; and under ordinary circumstances they support the nominees of the party to which they profess fealty. It is quite apparent that under such circumstances the primary election or caucus should be surrounded by such safeguards as will secure absolutely free and uncontrolled action. Here the people themselves are supposed to speak; here they put their own hands to the machinery of government, and in this place should be found the manifestations of the popular will. When by fraud, intimidation, or any other questionable practice the voice of the people is here smothered, a direct blow is aimed at a most precious right, and one which the law should be swift to protect. If the primary election is uncontaminated and fairly conducted, those there chosen to represent the people will go forth with the impress of the people's will upon them, and the benefits and purposes of a truly representative government will be attained.

Public officers are the servants and agents of the people to execute laws which the people have made, and within the limits of a constitution which they have established. Hence the interference of officials of any degree, and whether state or federal, for the purpose of thwarting or controlling the popular wish, should not be tolerated.

Subordinates in public place should be selected and retained for their efficiency, and not because they may be used to accomplish partisan ends. The people have a right to demand, here as in cases of private employment, that their money be paid to those who will render the best service in return, and that the appointment to and tenure of such places should depend upon ability and merit. If the clerks and assistants in public departments were paid the same compensation and required to do the same amount of work as those employed in prudently conducted private establishments, the anxiety to hold these public places would be much diminished, and, it seems to me, the cause of civil service reform materially aided.

The system of levying assessments for partisan purposes on those holding office or place cannot be too strongly condemned. Through the thin disguise of voluntary contributions, this is seen to be naked extortion, reducing the compensation which should be honestly earned, and swelling a fund used to debauch the people and defeat the popular will.

I am unalterably opposed to the interference by the Legislature with the government of municipalities. I believe in the intelligence of the people when left to an honest freedom in their choice, and that when the citizens of any section of the State have determined upon the details of a local government they should be left in the undisturbed enjoyment of the same. The doctrine of home rule, as I understand it, lies at the foundation of republican institutions, and cannot be too strongly insisted upon.

Corporations are created by the law for certain defined purposes and are restricted in their operations by specific limitations. Acting within their legitimate sphere, they should be protected; but when by combination or by the exercise of unwarranted power they oppress the people, the same authority which created should restrain them and protect the rights of the citizen. The law lately passed for the purpose of adjusting the relations between the people and corporations should be executed in good faith, with an honest design to effectuate its objects and with a due regard for the interest involved.

The laboring classes constitute the main part of our population. They should be protected in their efforts peaceably to assert their rights when endangered by aggregated capital, and all statutes on this subject should recognize the care of the State for honest toil and be framed with a view of improving the condition of the workingman.

We have so lately had a demonstration of the value of our citizen soldiery in time of peril that it seems to me no argument is necessary to prove that it should be maintained in a state of efficiency, so that its usefulness shall not be impaired.

Certain amendments to the Constitution of our State, involving the management of our canals, are to be passed upon at the coming election. This subject affects divers interests and of course gives rise to opposite opinions. It is in the hands of the sovereign people for final settlement; and, as the question is thus removed from State legislation, any statement of my opinion in regard to it, at this time, would, I think, be out of place. I am confident that the people will intelligently examine the merits of the subject and determine where the preponderance of interest lies.

The expenditure of money to influence the action of the people at the polls, or to secure legislation, is calculated to excite the gravest concern. When this pernicious agency is successfully employed, a representative form of government becomes a sham; and laws passed under its baleful influence cease to protect, but are made the means by which the rights of the people are sacrificed, and the public treasury despoiled. It is useless and foolish to shut our eyes to the fact that this evil exists among us; and the party which leads in an honest effort to return to better and purer methods will receive the confidence of our citizens and secure their support. It is wilful blindness not to see that the people care but little for party obligations, when they are invoked to countenance and sustain fraudulent and corrupt practices. And it is well for our country and for the purification of politics that the people, at times fully roused to danger, remind their leaders that party methods should be something more than a means used to answer the purposes of those who profit by political occupation.

The importance of wise statesmanship in the management of public affairs cannot, I think, be overestimated. I am convinced, however, that the perplexities and the mystery often surrounding the administration of State concerns grow, in a great measure, out of an attempt to serve partisan ends rather than the welfare of the citizen.

We may, I think, reduce to quite simple elements the duty which public servants owe, by constantly bearing in mind that they are put in place to protect the rights of the people, to answer their needs as they arise, and to expend for their benefit the money drawn from them by taxation.

I am profoundly conscious that the management of the divers interests of a great State is not an easy matter; but I believe, if undertaken in the proper spirit, all its real difficulties will yield to watchfulness and care.

Yours respectfully,
Grover Cleveland.

This admirable letter of acceptance attracted immediate attention, and the comments of the press on all sides were most favorable. The New York *Herald* expressed an editorial opinion as follows:—

There is something direct, fresh, and wholesome about this letter of Mr. Cleveland which encourages one to hope that the era of young men has really come, of which we have heard much this past summer. Anything more different from the usual platitudes of the old war-horses, to which the public has been too long accustomed, it would be difficult to imagine. Without the least air of dogmatism or any sniff of peculiar virtue, Mr. Cleveland briefly recalls to the public recollection a few facts which our political masters have for some years tried to have forgotten. For our own part we confess that the passage which strikes us as the most significant in the letter is that in which Mr. Cleveland writes: "I am convinced that the perplexities and the mystery often surrounding the administration of State concerns grow in a great measure out of an attempt to serve partisan ends rather than the welfare of the citizens. We may, I think, reduce to quite simple elements the duty which public servants owe by constantly bearing in mind that they are put in place to protect the rights of the people, to answer their needs as they arise, and to expend for their benefit the money drawn from them by taxation."

That is sound, clear, common-sense. There is no mystery or difficulty about free government, requiring great statesmanship or supereminent genius. Free government means at bottom the least possible interference with the liberty of action of the individual. It is a hopeful sign in our politics that a candidate for the great office of Governor of New York remembers this. It is natural that with this wholesome thought on his mind he should select for the topics on which he briefly touches mainly the questions which concern the correct ascertainment of the will of the people; the freedom and purity of primary elections, by which the people denote whom they wish to be candidates for office; the non-interference by public officers and corporations with the elections, hence the wrong of political assessments, used always in attempts to defeat the popular will; the necessity of local self government for the reform and purification of municipal administration, and so on.

There are no sounding promises, no recitals of recondite statesmanlike policies in this plain, blunt letter of Mr. Cleveland. But it reads to us like the letter of an intelligent American who has thought enough about free government to let him see that it needs in rulers mainly good sense, honesty, and courage, and who has no nonsense about him.

Upon the publication of the letter of acceptance, public opinion in the State of New York all went one way, political partisanship in a large measure disappeared and there was but one feeling, to secure the election of the best man. The Republicans of New York, with Stewart L. Woodford at the head, and Independents led by George William Curtis, all united in the support of the reform candidate for Governor. Thousands of Republicans led by the Young Men's Club of Brooklyn voted for Cleveland, and he swept the State like a tidal wave, carrying all before him. He was not elected solely by his party, but, as in his election for mayor, the Democratic vote was supplemented by that of every thinking man having the interests of his State at heart, without reference to partisan politics. He *was* Reform Mayor and Reform Governor and *is now* Reform President. Grover Cleveland took his office as Governor with the same simple manner that has always characterized him. His inaugural message had the true ring, and, being thoroughly characteristic of the man, we give space to such portions as are of the greatest importance.

THE INAUGURAL MESSAGE.

EXECUTIVE CHAMBER, ALBANY, January 2, 1883.

TO THE LEGISLATURE, — In obedience to the provisions of the Constitution, which directs that the Governor shall communicate to the Legislature, at every session, the condition of the State, and recommend such matters to them as he shall judge expedient, I transmit this, my first annual message, with the intimation that a newly elected executive can hardly be prepared to present a complete exhibit of State affairs, or to submit in detail a great variety of recommendations for the action of the Legislature. . . .

JUST AND EQUABLE TAXATION.

The aggregate receipts of the State Treasury during the last fiscal year, including a balance from the previous year amounting to $5,531,858.71, were $17,735,761.59; the payments during the same period amounted to $13,898,198.21, leaving a balance in the treasury at the beginning of the current fiscal year of $3,837,563.38.

The amount received from taxes on corporations during the last fiscal year was $1,539,684.27, being an increase of $446,959.11 over the previous year.

The rate of taxation for the current fiscal year was fixed by the last Legislature at $2\tfrac{45}{100}$ mills on the dollar. This, it is estimated, will yield, on the present valuation of property, a revenue of $6,820,022.29.

The imperfection of our laws touching the matter of taxation, or the faulty execution of existing statutes on the subject, is glaringly apparent.

The power of the State to exact from the citizen a part of his earnings and income for the support of the government, it is obvious, should be exercised with absolute fairness and justice. When it is not so exercised, the people are oppressed. This furnishes the highest and the best reason why laws should be enacted and executed, which will subject all property, as all alike need the protection of the State, to an equal share in the burdens of taxation, by means of which the government is maintained. And yet it is notoriously true that personal property, not less remunerative than land and real estate, escapes to a very great extent the payment of its fair proportion of the expense incident to its protection and preservation under the law. The people should always be able to recognize, with the pride and satisfaction which are the strength of our institutions, in the conduct of the State the source of undiscriminating justice, which can give no pretext for discontent. . . .

THE STATE PRISONS AND HONEST LABOR.

If these penal institutions are self-sustaining, without injury or embarrassment to honest labor, it is a matter for congratulation; but it is, at least, very questionable whether the State should go further and seek to realize a profit from its convict labor. In my judgment, it should not, especially if the danger of competition between convicts and those who honestly toil is thereby increased, and the overcrowding of any of the prisons, with its attendant evils, is the result. . . .

IMMIGRATION.

During the year the State Board of Charities has returned to various countries of Europe forty-eight lunatic, idiotic, crippled, blind, and otherwise disabled alien paupers, who had been deliberately shipped to our shores by the authorities of foreign cities and towns, or by relatives, guardians, and friends, in order to shift the burden of their support to our public charities. It is to be hoped that the continued return of such unfortunates to those who should legally and naturally provide for them will in time discourage such mean and disgraceful attempts to evade a plain and humane duty. . . .

CIVIL SERVICE REFORM.

It is submitted that the appointment of subordinates in the several State departments, and their tenure of office or employment, should be based upon fitness and efficiency, and that this principle should be embodied in legislative enactment, to the end that the policy of the State may conform to the reasonable public demand on that subject. . . .

CONCLUSION.

Let us enter upon the discharge of our duties fully appreciating our relations to the people, and determined to serve them faithfully and well. This involves a jealous watch of the public funds, and a refusal to sanction their appropriation except for public needs. To this end, all unnecessary offices should be abolished, and all employment of doubtful benefit discontinued. If to this we add the enactment of such wise and well considered laws as will meet the varied wants of our fellow-citizens, and increase their prosperity, we shall merit and receive the approval of those whose representatives we are, and, with the consciousness of duty well performed, shall leave our impress for good on the legislation of the State.

GROVER CLEVELAND.

So soon as he became Governor, Grover Cleveland commenced at once the work of reform, and did not confine it to large and important State questions, but began at home and in his immediate personal surroundings. A numerous body of useless men were discharged, and admission to see the Governor made free to all. He adopted a regular system of work, not only for his employés but also for his own office, and no official in his department did as much work as the Governor himself. His attention was directed to the subject of pardons, the decision upon which had heretofore been in the hands of a pardon clerk, and he at once assumed the responsibility of the examination and decision upon all pardons himself. He was especially anxious to give proper attention to all that related to the amelioration of the condition of laboring men, and through the fearless use of his veto power he prevented the enactment into statutes of several measures which would have been injurious to the workingmen. Under his administration a State Civil Service Reform bill and a bill prohibiting political assessments were passed and signed by the Governor. A bureau of labor statistics was also established with his approval, and with results of great advantage to the State. Many attacks were made upon Grover Cleveland having special reference to his views upon the labor question, and, when an attempt was made to defeat his nomination at a subsequent date, he said : —

To say that I have ever failed to embrace every opportunity offered me to elevate the condition and subserve the real interests of the workingman, and to protect him in all his rights, is false. This, however, is but evidence of the readiness of some persons to make careless statements when engaged in a struggle, and of others to accept such statements as facts instead of ascertaining the truth from the record. Understand me ; I do not profess to be infallible on this or any other question, but I do claim that no sincere and honest workingman can examine my record and find from it anything which tends to show a lack of sympathy with and care for the true interests of those who labor. I am sometimes afraid that at least a few of those who pose as friends of the workingmen do not keep themselves fully informed as to what is done for them by way of legislation. As an illustration, I see it stated in the papers, as coming from one who professes to be especially the friend of the workingmen, and claiming to be a leader among them, that I vetoed a bill preventing contract labor by children in the reformatories and institutions of the State. In point of fact, this bill was promptly signed by me, and no other measure touching this question has been presented to me.

Governor Cleveland's veto of the Elevated Railroad five-cent fare bill was occasion of universal clamor, simply from the fact of its not being generally understood. We give herewith the last clauses of his veto message, which cover his most important views on the subject: —

It is manifestly important that invested capital should be protected, and that its necessity and usefulness in the development of enterprises valuable to the people should be recognized by conservative conduct on the part of the State government.

But we have especially in our keeping the honor and good faith of a great State, and we should see to it that no suspicion attaches, through any act of ours, to the fair fame of the commonwealth. The State should not only be strictly just, but scrupulously fair, and in its relations to the citizens every legal and moral obligation should be recognized. This can only be done by legislating without vindictiveness or prejudice, and with a firm determination to deal justly and fairly with those from whom we exact obedience.

I am not unmindful of the fact that this bill originated in response to the demand of a large portion of the people of New York for cheaper rates of fare between their places of employment and their homes, and I realize fully the desirability of securing to them all the privileges possible, but the experience of other States teaches that we must keep within the limits of law and good faith, lest in the end we bring upon the very people whom we seek to benefit and protect a hardship which must surely follow when these limits are ignored.

GROVER CLEVELAND.

That we may form some idea of the impression made upon thinking men by this message, we give herewith a letter from Rev. Dr. Anderson, president of Rochester University, and one of our most prominent educators: —

ROCHESTER, March 4, 1883.

GOVERNOR CLEVELAND : —

Sir, — I cannot, in justice to my convictions, refrain from expressing my gratitude for your veto message, which I have just read. I have no personal interest in any of the great corporations which were directly or indirectly affected by the bill from which you have so wisely withheld your approval. But the just and statesmanlike position taken in your message seems to me a most fitting rebuke to the demagogism which is ready to trifle with those sacred rights of property guaranteed by our State and national constitutions. In these safeguards of property the poor man has a more vital interest than the capitalist, for they make secure the poor man's savings, which constitute his only means of support. I have taken occasion to commend your message to the careful consideration of my students, as an exhibition of the principles which should govern their actions should they be called to fill public station in their future lives. I trust you will pardon me for obtruding myself upon your attention. As a teacher of young men, I feel grateful to any public functionary who illustrates in his person the lessons which I am so anxious to impress upon their minds. Again I thank you for the courageous and worthy action which you have adopted to secure sound government for our great State.

Yours very respectfully,
MARTIN B. ANDERSON.

The second year of Grover Cleveland's administration as Governor of the Empire State commenced under the best auspices; he had secured the approval and good-will of five millions of people, who were perfectly satisfied with his control of the government. His second inaugural message dwelt on many local subjects of great interest, but space will not permit us to present but such as seem worthy of special attention at the present time.

The Governor said as follows in reference to

CIVIL SERVICE. REFORM.

During the year the provisions of the act passed by the last Legislature to regulate and improve the civil service of the State have been put into operation. Fortunately a commission was secured whose members were in hearty sympathy with the principles of the law, and who possessed much practical knowledge of the needs of the public service. The commission itself was also fortunate in obtaining the services of Silas W. Burt as chief examiner, whose experience in public affairs and familiarity with the best methods of regulating the civil service enabled him to render invaluable assistance to the commission and the State. The preliminary classification and the framing of rules, contemplated by the act governing the appointments to place, having been completed and received my approval, the system will become operative in respect to all State officers and in all State institutions on the fourth day of the present month. This work, owing to the diversity of the State service, and the number and variety of positions affected by the law, has been a task attended with many difficulties. Although some slight revision may be necessary, on the whole I am confident the scheme will be found practical and effective, without being too rigorous or burdensome.

In addition the commission has co-operated with the mayors of cities who, under the law, have exclusive control of the municipal service, and in several cities, notably New York and Brooklyn, a thorough system of civil service has been prepared and promulgated, as nearly in harmony with the State system as the charters and statutes relating to municipal matters will permit.

New York, then, leads in the inauguration of a comprehensive State system of civil service. The principle of selecting the subordinate employés of the State on the ground of capacity and fitness, ascertained according to fixed and impartial rules, without regard to political predilections, and with reasonable assurance of retention and promotion in case of meritorious service, is now the established policy of the State. The children of our citizens are educated and trained in schools maintained at common expense, and the people as a whole have a right to demand the selection for the public service of those whose natural aptitudes have been improved by the educational facilities furnished by the State. The application to the public service of the same rule which prevails in ordinary business, of employing those whose knowledge and training best fit them for the duties at hand, without regard to other considerations, must elevate and improve the civil service and eradicate from it many evils from which it has long suffered. Not the least gratifying of the results which this system promises to accomplish is relief to public men from the annoyance of importunity in the strife for appointments to subordinate places.

RESULTS OF THE FIRST YEAR.

The people of the State are to be congratulated upon the progress made during the last year in the direction of wholesome legislation.

The most practical and thorough civil service reform has gained a place in the policy of the State.

Political assessments upon employés in the public departments have been prohibited.

The rights of all citizens at primary elections have been protected by law.

A bureau has been established to collect information and statistics touching the relations between labor and capital.

The sale of forest land at the source of our important streams has been prohibited, thereby checking threatened disaster to the commerce on our waterways.

Debts and obligations for the payment of money, owned though not actually held within the State, have been made subject to taxation, thus preventing an unfair evasion of liability for the support of the government.

Business principles have been introduced in the construction and care of the new capitol and other public buildings, and waste and extravagance thereby prevented.

A law has been passed for the better administration of the Emigration Bureau and the prevention of its abuses.

The people have been protected by placing coöperative insurance companies under the control and supervision of the Insurance Department.

The fees of receivers have been reduced and regulated in the interests of the creditors of insolvent companies.

A court of claims has been established where the demands of citizens against the State may be properly determined.

These legislative accomplishments, and others of less importance and prominence, may well be cited in proof of the fact that the substantial interests of the people of the State have not been neglected.

. . . . .

Let us anticipate a time when care for the people's needs as they actually arise, and the application of remedies, as wrongs appear, shall lead in the conduct of national affairs; and let us undertake the business of legislation with the full determination that these principles shall guide us in the performance of our duties as guardians of the interests of the State.

GROVER CLEVELAND.

The vetoes of Governor Cleveland during the session of the Legislature of 1884 attracted much carping opposition, but, as usual, when the good commonsense of the people fairly considered his views, he was almost unanimously supported, and it must be admitted that as Governor he consistently carried out the same ideas of reform and correction of financial abuses that he did in his capacity of mayor of Buffalo.

THE EXECUTIVE MANSION, WASHINGTON, D.C.

CHAPTER IV.

GROVER CLEVELAND AS PRESIDENT.

As a natural result, the admirable administration of Grover Cleveland as Governor of the Empire State led to the early consideration of his name in connection with the Democratic nomination for the Presidency in 1884. He had made a good mayor, he had made a good Governor, he should make a good President. So soon as Governor Tilden declined the nomination, prominent Democrats at once came out in favor of Cleveland, among them ex-Governor Horatio Seymour and ex-Senator Francis Kernan. At the Democratic State Convention held at Saratoga, the delegation to the national convention were instructed to give their unanimous vote for Grover Cleveland.

The Democratic National Convention met at Chicago on July 8, 1884, Colonel William F. Vilas, of Wisconsin, being appointed permanent chairman. The name of Grover Cleveland was presented by Mr. Daniel S. Lockwood, of Buffalo, representing the delegation from the State of New York. The remarks of Mr. Lockwood, made four years since, are so patent to the present occasion that they are given here in full:—

Mr. Chairman and Gentlemen of the Convention: It is with no ordinary feeling of responsibility that I appear before this convention, as representative of the Democracy of the State of New York, for the purpose of placing in nomination a gentleman from the State of New York, as a candidate for the Presidency of the United States. This responsibility is made greater when I remember that the richest pages of American history have been made up from the records of Democratic administration. This responsibility is made still greater when I remember that the only blot in the political history done at Washington, an outrage upon the rights of the American people, was in 1876, and that that outrage and that injury to justice is still unavenged, and this responsibility is not lessened when I recall the fact that the gentleman whose name I shall present to you has been my political associate from my youth. Side by side have we marched to the tune of Democratic music; side by side we studied the principles of Jefferson and Jackson, and we love the faith in which we believe; and during all this time he has occupied a position comparatively as a private citizen, yet always true and always faithful to Democratic principle. No man has greater respect or admiration for the honored names which have been presented to this convention than myself; but, gentlemen, the world is moving, and moving rapidly.

From the North to the South, new men — men who have acted but little in politics — are coming to the front, and to-day there are hundreds and thousands of young men in this country — men who are to cast their first vote, who are independent in politics — and they are looking to this convention, praying silently that there shall be no mistake made here. They want to drive the Republican party from power; they want to cast their vote for a Democrat in whom they believe. These people know from the record of the gentleman whose name I shall present, that Democracy with him means honest government, pure government, and protection of the rights of the people of every class and every condition. A little more than three years ago, I had the honor, at the city of Buffalo, to present the name of this same gentleman for the office of mayor of that city. It was presented then for the same reason, for the same causes that we present it now; it was because the government of that city had become corrupt and had become debauched, and political integrity sat not in high places. The people looked for a man who would represent the contrary, and without any hesitation they named Grover Cleveland as the man. The result of that election, and his holding that office, was that in less than nine months the State of New York found herself in a position to want just such a candidate and for such a purpose, and when, at the convention in 1882, his name was placed in nomination for the office of Governor of the State of New York, the same people, the same class of people, knew that that meant honest government, it meant pure government, it meant Democratic government, and it was ratified by the people. And, gentlemen, now, after eighteen months' service there, the Democracy of the State of New York come to you and ask you to give to the country, to give the independent and Democratic voters of the country, the new blood of the country, and present the name of Grover Cleveland as its standard-bearer for the next four years. I shall indulge in no eulogy of Mr. Cleveland. I shall not attempt any further description of his political career. It is known. His Democracy is known. His statesmanship is known throughout the length and breadth of this land. And all I ask of this convention is to let no passion, no prejudice, influence its duty which it owes to the people of this country. Be not deceived. Grover Cleveland can give the Democratic party the thirty-six electoral votes of the State of New York on election day. He can, by his purity of character, by his purity of administration, by his fearless and undaunted courage to do right, bring to you more votes than anybody else. Gentlemen of the convention, but one word more. Mr. Cleveland's candidacy before this convention is offered upon the ground of his honor, his integrity, his wisdom, and his Democracy. Upon that ground we ask it, believing that if ratified by this convention he can be elected and take his seat at Washington as a Democratic President of the United States.

Upon the second ballot taken in the convention the name of Grover Cleveland was adopted as Democratic candidate for President by a vote which was at once made unanimous, the formal announcement of the vote being: —

Cleveland 683
Bayard 81½
Hendricks 45½
Thurman 4
Randall 4
McDonald 2

In detail the States voted as follows: —

STATES.	Delegates.	Cleveland.	McDonald.	Bayard.	Thurman.	Hendricks.	Randall.
Alabama	20	5	1	14			
Arkansas	14	14					
California	16	16					
Colorado	6	6					
Connecticut	12	12					
Delaware	6			6			
Florida	8	8					
Georgia	24	22		2			
Illinois	44	43	1				
Indiana	30	30					
Iowa	26	26					
Kansas	18	17		1			
Kentucky	26	4		21	1		
Louisiana	16	15			1		
Maine	12	12					
Maryland	16	16					
Massachusetts	28	8		7½		12½	
Michigan	26	23				3	
Minnesota	14	14					
Mississippi	18	2		14		2	
Missouri	32	32					
Nebraska	10	9		1			
Nevada	6				1	5	
New Hampshire	8	8					
New Jersey	18	5		2		11	
New York	72	72					

STATES.	Delegates.	Cleveland.	McDonald.	Bayard.	Thurman.	Hendricks.	Randall.
North Carolina	22	22	..	..	..	..	..
Ohio	46	46	..	..	..	..	..
Oregon	6	6	..	..	..	..	..
Pennsylvania	60	42	..	3	1	11	4
Rhode Island	8	7	..	2	..	..	..
South Carolina	18	10	..	8	..	..	..
Tennessee	24	24	..	..	..	..	..
Texas	26	26	..	..	..	..	..
Vermont	8	8	..	..	..	..	..
Virginia	24	23	..	..	..	1	..
West Virginia	12	10	..	2	..	..	..
Wisconsin	22	22	..	..	..	..	..
Arizona	2	2	..	..	..	..	..
Dakota	2	2	..	..	..	..	..
Idaho	2	2	..	..	..	..	..
Montana	2	2	..	..	..	..	..
New Mexico	2	2	..	..	..	..	..
Utah	2	2	..	..	..	..	..
Washington	2	2	..	..	..	..	..
Wyoming	2	2	..	..	..	..	..
District of Columbia	2	2	..	..	..	..	..
Totals	820	683	2	$81\frac{1}{2}$	4	$45\frac{1}{2}$	4

Governor Cleveland was quietly at work at his regular executive routine of business when the news arrived of his nomination, and he was at once obliged to receive the congratulations of his friends and fellow-countrymen. In reply to an address by Mr. James Tracey, President of the Young Men's Club, Governor Cleveland said: —

FELLOW-CITIZENS, — I cannot but be gratified with this kindly greeting. I find that I am fast reaching the point where I shall count the people of Albany not merely as fellow-citizens, but as townsmen and neighbors.

On this occasion I am, of course, aware that you pay no compliment to a citizen, and present no personal tribute, but that you have come to demonstrate your loyalty and devotion to a cause in which you are heartily enlisted.

The American people are about to exercise, in its highest sense, their power and right of sovereignty. They are to call in review before them their public servants and the representatives of political parties, and demand of them an account of their stewardship.

Parties may be so long in power, and may become so arrogant and careless of the interests of the people, as to grow heedless of their responsibility to their masters. But the time comes, as certainly as death, when the people weigh them in the balance.

The issues to be adjudicated by the nation's great assize are made up and are about to be submitted.

We believe that the people are not receiving, at the hands of the party which for nearly twenty-four years has directed the affairs of the nation, the full benefits to which they are entitled, of a pure, just, and economical rule; and we bel'eve that the ascendency of genuine Democratic principles will insure a better government, and greater happiness and prosperity to all the people.

To reach the sober thought of the nation, and to dislodge an enemy intrenched behind spoils and patronage, involve a struggle which if we underestimate we invite defeat. I am profoundly impressed with the responsibility of the part assigned to me in this contest. My heart, I know, is in the cause, and I pledge you that no effort of mine shall be wanting to secure the victory which I believe to be within the achievement of the Democratic hosts.

Let us, then, enter upon the campaign now fairly opened, each one appreciating well the part he has to perform, ready, with solid front, to do battle for better government, confidently, courageously, always honorably, and with a firm reliance upon the intelligence and patriotism of the American people.

At the conclusion of his remarks the audience cheered again and again tumultuously as the Governor reëntered the house. The doors were thrown open, and, taking his place in the broad hallway, on the spot where eight years before Governor Tilden had received the congratulations of the people on his nomination, Governor Cleveland shook hands with the thousands who for two hours poured steadily in one door and out the other.

Governor Cleveland was officially notified of his nomination to the high office of President of the United States in the afternoon of July 29, 1884. The ceremony took place in the Governor's mansion. Colonel Vilas, president of the notification committee delivered the following address : —

GROVER CLEVELAND, GOVERNOR OF THE STATE OF NEW YORK, — These gentlemen, my associates here present, whose voice I am honored with authority to utter, are a committee appointed by the National Democratic Convention which recently assembled in Chicago, and charged with the grateful duty of acquainting you, officially and in that solemn and ceremonious manner which the dignity and importance of the communication demand, with the interesting result of its deliberations, already known to you through the ordinary channels of news.

Sir, the august body, convened by direct delegation from the Democratic people of the several States and Territories of the republic, and deliberating under the witness of the greatest assembly of freemen ever gathered to such a conference, in forethought of the election which the Constitution imposes upon them to make during the current year, have nominated you to the people of these United States to be their President for the next ensuing term of that great office, and, with grave consideration of its exalted responsibilities, have confidently invoked their suffrages to invest you with its functions. Through this committee the convention's high requirement is delivered that you accept that candidacy.

This choice carries with it profound personal respect and admiration; but it has been in no manner the fruit of these sentiments. The national Democracy seek a President not in compliment for what the man is, or reward for what he has done, but in a just expectation of what he will accomplish as the true servant of a free people, fit for their lofty trust. Always of momentous consequence, they conceive the public exigency to be now of transcendent importance, that a laborious reform in administration, as well as legislation, is imperatively necessary to the prosperity and honor of the republic, and a competent chief magistrate must be of unusual temper and power. They have observed with attention your execution of the public trusts you have held, especially of that with which you are now so honorably invested.

They place their reliance for the usefulness of the services they expect to exact for the benefit of the nation upon the evidence derived from the services you have performed for the State of New York. They invite the electors to such proofs of character and competence to justify their confidence that in the nation, as heretofore in the State, the public business will be administered with commensurate intelligence and ability, with single-hearted honesty and fidelity, and with a resolute and daring fearlessness which no faction, no combination, no power of wealth, no mistaken clamor, can dismay or qualify.

In the spirit of the wisdom and invoking the benediction of the Divine Teacher of men, we challenge from the sovereignty of this nation his words in commendation and ratification of our choice, "Well done, thou good and faithful servant; thou hast been faithful over a few things, I will make thee ruler over many things." In further fulfilment of our duty, the secretary will now present the written communication signed by the committee.

Governor Cleveland remained calm throughout these remarks and looked the speaker squarely in the face. Mr. Bell, the secretary of the committee, then read the letter of notification, afterward handing the manuscript, inclosed in its leather wallet, to the Governor.

Following is the address of the committee of notification:—

NEW YORK CITY, July 28, 1884.
To the Hon. GROVER CLEVELAND, of New York: —

Sir, — In accordance with a custom befitting the nature of the communication, the undersigned, representing the several States and Territories of the Union, were appointed a committee by the National Democratic Convention, which assembled at Chicago, on the eighth day of the current month, to perform the pleasing office which by this means we have the honor to execute, of informing you of your nomination as the candidate of the Democratic party in the ensuing election for the office of President of the United States. A declaration of the principles upon which the Democracy go before the people with the hope of establishing and maintaining them in the government was made by the convention, and an engrossed copy thereof is submitted in connection with this communication for your consideration. We trust the approval of your judgment will follow an examination of this expression of opinion and policy, and upon the political controversy now made up we invite your acceptance of the exalted leadership to which you have been chosen.

The election of a President is an event of the utmost importance to the people of America. Prosperity, growth, happiness, peace, and liberty even may depend upon its wise ordering. Your unanimous nomination is proof that the Democracy believe your election will most contribute to secure these great objects. We assure you that in the anxious responsibilities you must assume as a candidate you will have the steadfast, cordial support of the friends of the cause you will represent, and, in the execution of the duties of the high office which we confidently expect from the wisdom of the nation to be conferred upon you, you may securely rely for approving aid upon the patriotism, honor, and intelligence of this free people. We have the honor to be, with great respect,

W. F. VILAS (Wisconsin), President.
NICHOLAS N. BELL (Missouri), Secretary.

D. P. BESTOR, Ala.,
FRED. W. FORDYCE, Ark.,
NILES SEARLES, Cal.,
M. M. S. WALLER, Col.,
THEO. M. WALLER, Conn.,
GEORGE H. BATES, Del.,
ATILLA COX, Ky.,
JAMES JEFFRIES, La.,
D. E. MCCARTHY, Nev.,
J. F. CLOUTMAN, N. H.,
JOHN P. STOCKTON, N. J.,
JOHN C. JACOBS, N. Y.,
G. H. OURY, Arizona,
RANSFORD SMITH, Utah,
JOHN M. SELCOTT, Idaho,
W. D. CHIPLEY, Fla.,

C. H. Osgood, Me.,
George Wells, Md.,
J. E. Abbott, Mass.,
D. J. Campan, Mich.,
Thos. E. Heenan, Minn.,
Charles E. Hooker, Miss.,
David R. Francis, Mo.,
Patrick Fahy, Neb.,
Wilson G. Lamb, N. C.,
Joseph H. Earle, S. C.,
Wm. A. Quarles, Tenn.,
George L. Spear, Vt.,
Frank Hereford, W. Va.,
J. T. Hauser, Montana,
M. S. McCormick, D. T.,
M. P. Reese, Ga.,
A. E. Stevenson, Ill.,
E. D. Bannister, Ind.,
L. G. Kinne, Iowa,
C. C. Burnes, Kan.,
Wm. E. Haynes, Ohio,
S. L. McArthur, Ore.,
James P. Barr, Pa.,
David S. Baker, Jr., R. I.,
E. D. Wright, Dist. of Col.,
Joseph E. Dwyer, Texas,
Robert Beverly, Va.,
W. A. Anderson, Wis.,
W. B. Childers, N. Mex.,
D. B. Dutro, W. T.

Governor Cleveland received the proffered wallet gracefully and replied quietly, without gesture and without the use of manuscript : —

Mr. Chairman and Gentlemen of the Committee, — Your formal announcement does not, of course, convey to me the first information of the result of the convention lately held by the Democracy of the nation, and yet when, as I listen to your message, I see about me representatives from all parts of the land of the great party which, claiming to be the party of the people, asks them to intrust to it the administration of their government; and when I consider, under the influence of the stern reality which the present surroundings create, that I have been chosen to represent the plans, purposes, and the policy of the Democratic party, I am profoundly impressed by the solemnity of the occasion and by the responsibility of my position.

Though I gratefully appreciate it, I do not at this moment congratulate myself upon the distinguished honor which has been conferred upon me, because my mind is full of an anxious desire to perform well the part which has been assigned to me. Nor do I at this moment forget that the rights and interests of more than fifty millions of my fellow-citizens are involved in our efforts to gain Democratic supremacy. This reflection presents to my mind the consideration which more than all others gives to the action of my party in convention assembled its most sober and serious aspect. The party and its representatives which ask to be intrusted at the hands of the people with the keeping of all that concerns their welfare and their safety should only ask it with the full appreciation of the sacredness of the trust and with a firm resolve to administer it faithfully and well. I am a Democrat because I believe that this truth lies at the foundation of true democracy. I have kept the faith because I believe, if rightly and fairly administered and applied, Democratic doctrines and measures will insure the happiness, contentment, and prosperity of the people.

If, in the contest upon which we now enter, we steadfastly hold to the underlying principles of our party creed, and at all times keep in view the people's good, we shall be strong, because we are true to ourselves and because the plain and independent voters of the land will seek by their suffrages to compass their release from party tyranny where there should be submission to the popular will, and their protection from party corruption where there should be devotion to the people's interests. These thoughts lend a consecration to our cause, and we go forth not merely to gain a partisan advantage, but pledged to give to those who trust us the utmost benefits of a pure and honest administration of national affairs. No higher purpose or motive can stimulate us to supreme effort or urge us to continuous and earnest labor and effective party organization. Let us not fail in this, and we may confidently hope to reap the full reward of patriotic services well performed.

I have thus called to mind some simple truths, and, trite though they are, it seems to me we do well to dwell upon them at this time. I shall soon, I hope, signify in the usual formal manner my acceptance of the nomination which has been tendered me. In the meantime I gladly greet you all as co-workers in a noble cause.

The reply of Grover Cleveland to the letter from the committee announcing his nomination is a simple restatement of his views as expressed heretofore, with the results of his added experience as mayor and Governor. His views as regards the executive management of the administration of a great nation have been faithfully carried out during the past three years, and the reader who follows carefully all of its utterances will be surprised at their almost exact confirmation by the acts of the President.

LETTER OF ACCEPTANCE.

ALBANY, N. Y., August 18, 1884.

GENTLEMEN,—I have received your communication, dated July 28, 1884, informing me of my nomination to the office of President of the United States, by the National Democratic Convention lately assembled at Chicago.

I accept the nomination with a grateful appreciation of the supreme honor conferred, and a solemn sense of the responsibility which, in its acceptance, I assume.

I have carefully considered the platform adopted by the convention, and cordially approve the same. So plain a statement of Democratic faith and the principles upon which that party appeals to the suffrages of the people needs no supplement or explanation.

It should be remembered that the office of President is essentially executive in its nature. The laws enacted by the legislative branch of the government the chief executive is bound faithfully to enforce. And when the wisdom of the political party which selects one of its members as a nominee for that office has outlined its policy and declared its principles, it seems to me that nothing in the character of the office or the necessities of the case requires more from the candidate accepting such nomination than the suggestion of certain well known truths, so absolutely vital to the safety and welfare of the nation that they cannot be too often recalled or too seriously enforced.

GOVERNMENT BY THE PEOPLE.

We proudly call ours a government by the people. It is not such when a class is tolerated which arrogates to itself the management of public affairs, seeking to control the people instead of representing them.

Parties are the necessary outgrowth of our institutions, but a government is not by the people when one party fastens its control upon the country and perpetuates its power by cajoling and betraying the people instead of serving them.

A government is not by the people when a result which

should represent the intelligent will of free and thinking men is or can be determined by the shameless corruption of their suffrages.

When an election to office shall be the selection by the voters of one of their number, to assume for a time a public trust instead of his dedication to the profession of politics; when the holders of the ballot, quickened by a sense of duty, shall avenge truth betrayed and pledges broken, and when the suffrage shall be altogether free and uncorrupted, the full realization of a government by the people will be at hand. And of the means to this end not one would, in my judgment, be more effective than an amendment to the constitution disqualifying the President from reëlection. When we consider the patronage of this great office, the allurements of power, the temptation to retain public place once gained, and, more than all, the availability a party finds in an incumbent whom a horde of office-holders, with a zeal born of benefits received and fostered by the hope of favors yet to come, stand ready to aid with money and trained political service, we recognize in the eligibility of the President for reelection a most serious danger to that calm, deliberate, and intelligent political action which must characterize a government by the people.

LABOR MUST BE PROTECTED.

A true American sentiment recognizes the dignity of labor and the fact that honor lies in honest toil. Contented labor is an element of national prosperity. Ability to work constitutes the capital and the wage of labor, the income of a vast number of our population, and this interest should be jealously protected. Our workingmen are not asking unreasonable indulgence, but as intelligent and manly citizens they seek the same consideration which those demand who have other interests at stake. They should receive their full share of the care and attention of those who make and execute the laws, to the end that the wants and needs of the employers and the employed shall alike be subserved, and the prosperity of the country, the common heritage of both, be advanced. As related to this subject, while we should not discourage the immigration of those who come to acknowledge allegiance to our government and add to our citizen population, yet, as a means of protection to our workingmen, a different rule should prevail concerning those who, if they come or are brought to our land, do not intend to become Americans, but will injuriously compete with those justly entitled to our field of labor.

In a letter accepting the nomination to the office of Governor, nearly two years ago, I made the following statement, to which I have steadily adhered: —

"The laboring classes constitute the main part of our population. They should be protected in their efforts peaceably to assert their rights when endangered by aggregated capital, and all statutes on this subject should recognize the care of the State for honest toil, and be framed with a view of improving the condition of the workingman."

A proper regard for the welfare of the workingman being inseparably connected with the integrity of our institutions, none of our citizens are more interested than they in guarding against any corrupting influences which seek to pervert the beneficent purposes of our government, and none should be more watchful of the artful machinations of those who allure them to self-inflicted injury.

CONSERVATION OF INDIVIDUAL RIGHTS.

In a free country the curtailment of the absolute rights of the individual should only be such as is essential to the peace and good order of the community. The limit between the proper subjects of governmental control and those which can be more fittingly left to the moral sense and self-imposed restraint of the citizen should be carefully kept in view. Thus, laws unnecessarily interfering with the habits and customs of any of our people, which are not offensive to the moral sentiments of the civilized world, and which are consistent with good citizenship and the public welfare, are unwise and vexatious.

The commerce of a nation, to a great extent, determines its supremacy. Cheap and easy transportation should therefore be liberally fostered. Within the limits of the constitution, the general government should so improve and protect its natural waterways as will enable the producers of the country to reach a profitable market.

THE PUBLIC SERVICE.

The people pay the wages of the public employés, and they are entitled to the fair and honest work which the money thus paid should command. It is the duty of those intrusted with the management of their affairs to see that such public service is forthcoming. The selection and retention of subordinates in government employment should depend upon their ascertained fitness and the value of their work, and they should be neither expected nor allowed to do questionable party service. The interests of the people will be better protected; the estimate of public labor and duty will be immensely improved; public employment will be open to all who can demonstrate their fitness to enter it; the unseemly scramble for place under the government, with the consequent importunity which embitters official life, will cease; and the public departments will not be filled with those who conceive it to be their first duty to aid the party to which they owe their places, instead of rendering patient and honest return to the people.

AN HONEST ADMINISTRATION WANTED.

I believe that the public temper is such that the voters of the land are prepared to support the party which gives the best promise of administering the government in the honest, simple, and plain manner which is consistent with its character and purposes. They have learned that mystery and concealment in the management of their affairs cover tricks and betrayal. The statesmanship they require consists in honesty and frugality, a prompt response to the needs of the people as they arise, and the vigilant protection of all their varied interests.

If I should be called to the chief magistracy of the nation by the suffrages of my fellow-citizens, I will assume the duties of that high office with a solemn determination to dedicate every effort to the country's good, and with an humble reliance upon the favor and support of the Supreme Being, who, I believe, will always bless honest human endeavor in the conscientious discharge of public duty.

GROVER CLEVELAND

To Colonel WILLIAM F. VILAS, Chairman, and D. P. BESTOR, and others, Members of the Notification Committee of the Democratic National Convention.

The nomination of Grover Cleveland was accepted by the press of all parties as the best thing for the nation's good, and Democrat, Republican, and Independent joined hands in praise of the man so unexpectedly brought forward. Geo. Wm. Curtis, in *Harper's Weekly*, refused to countenance the Republican ticket, and published the following leading editorial: —

> The nomination of Grover Cleveland defines sharply the actual issue of the presidential election of this year. He is a man whose absolute official integrity has never been questioned, who has no laborious and doubtful explanations to undertake, and who is universally known as the Governor of New York, elected by an unprecedented majority which was not partisan, and represented both the votes and the consent of an enormous body of Republicans, and who, as the chief executive of the State, has steadily withstood the blandishments and the threats of the worst elements of his party, and has justly earned the reputation of a courageous, independent, and efficient friend and promoter of administrative reform. His name has become that of the especial representative among our public men of the integrity, purity, and economy of administration which are the objects of the most intelligent and patriotic citizens. The bitter and furious hostility of Tammany Hall and of General Butler to Governor Cleveland is his passport to the confidence of good men, and the general conviction that Tammany will do all that it can to defeat him will be an additional incentive to the voters who cannot support Mr. Blaine, and who are unwilling not to vote at all, to secure the election of a candidate whom the political rings and the party traders instinctively hate and unitedly oppose.
>
> So firm and "clean" and independent in his high office has Governor Cleveland shown himself to be that he is denounced as not being a Democrat by his Democratic opponents. This denunciation springs from the fact that he has not hesitated to prefer the public welfare to the mere interest of his party. Last autumn, when the Democratic district attorney of Queen's County was charged with misconduct, the Governor heard the

accusation and the defence, and decided that it was his duty to remove the officer. He was asked by his party friends to defer the removal until after the election, as otherwise the party would lose the district by the opposition of the attorney's friends. The Governor understood his duty, and removed the officer some days before the election, and the party did lose the district. This kind of courage and devotion to public duty in the teeth of the most virulent opposition of traders of his own party is unusual in any public man, and it shows precisely the executive quality which is demanded at a time when every form of speculation and fraud presses upon the public treasury under the specious plea of party advantage..

The argument that in an election it is not a man but a party that is supported, and that the Democratic party is less to be trusted than the Republican, is futile at a time when the Republican party has nominated a candidate whom a great body of the most conscientious Republicans cannot support, and the Democratic party has nominated a candidate whom a great body of the most venal Democrats practically bolt. Distrust of the Democratic party springs from the conduct of the very Democrats who madly oppose Governor Cleveland because they know that they cannot use him. The mere party argument is vain also because no honorable man will be whipped in to vote for a candidate whom he believes to be personally disqualified for the presidency on the ground that a party ought to be sustained. No honest Republican would sustain his party for such a reason, and the honest Republicans who propose to vote for Mr. Blaine will do so because they do not believe, as the protesting Republicans do believe, that he made his official action subserve a personal advantage. Nothing is more hopeless than an attempt to persuade such Republicans to sustain their party by voting for an unworthy candidate. Should they help to reward such a candidate by conferring upon him the highest official honor in the world, they could not reasonably expect the nomination of a worthier candidate at the next election, and they could not consistently oppose the election of any candidate whom their party might select. The time to defeat unfit nominations is when they are made, not next time. The nomination of Governor Cleveland is due not so much to the preference of his party as to the general demand of the country for a candidacy which stands for precisely the qualities and services which are associated with his name.

The New York *Times*, formerly a strong *Republican* organ, appeared the next day after the nomination with this argument: —

> With Governor Cleveland as its candidate the Democratic party appeals with unmistakable directness to the moral sense of the people of the United States. Shall the next President be a man who has weakly yielded to temptation or a man who has unswervingly adhered to the right against powerful enticements to do wrong? A man who begs pecuniary rewards of those his official action has enriched, or one who defies corrupt dictation and seeks only by just courses to deserve the approval of right-thinking men? A candidate attacked, impeached, tainted, and besmirched all over, or a candidate beyond reproach? A Grover Cleveland, whom honest men respect, or a James G. Blaine, whom rogues love?
>
> This is the supreme issue. It is this which the voters of the republic are to decide. It is not the issue of protection; free trade has nothing to do with it; there is no admixture of foreign policy or the want of foreign policy; insincere professions cannot put it aside; the glare of a boasted torchlight brilliancy will not outshine it. The sober sense of an intelligent electorate, the honest convictions and the patriotism of ten millions of voters are appealed to, and they will settle this question conclusively and for the right.
>
> It is not only in what he clearly represents, but in what he distinctly opposes, that Grover Cleveland is strong before the American people. His career has made him the exponent of clean and honest politics. In the administration of public trusts he has shown that he is superior to partisan bias, indifferent to such party interests as are in conflict with official probity and the public welfare. He has been severely tried in the important and responsible post he now occupies. He has resisted the importunities of designing politicians, he has defeated the purposes of selfish schemers. All those members of his own party who are not absorbed in private aims which are in conflict with the public good are outspoken in his praise; and he has won the good opinion of all Republicans who are not so far gone in partisanship as to have lost the power to commend upright conduct in a political adversary.

Favored as he is by the right-thinking elements of both the Democratic and Republican parties, it is a noteworthy and potent advantage to Grover Cleveland as a candidate that he has incurred the bitter hostility of the worthless, disreputable, and dangerous members of his own party. Tammany hates him. Butler sees no good in him. Could a candidate find stronger recommendation than this in the opinion of voters whose political action is shaped solely by considerations of public welfare? The official acts which have won for Governor Cleveland the intense hostility of Tammany are the very acts which have most strongly commended him to the support of independent Republicans. The favor of these two classes, of a wholly corrupt and selfish guerilla contingent within the Democratic party, and of men with whom plain common sense and the most ordinary form of political honesty are controlling influences, no one man, be he ever so skilful in the art of balancing, can hope or wish to possess. Grover Cleveland had not been one month in office as Governor of the State of New York before he had decided in his own mind and had made plain to all observers that his official action was to be guided solely by his own intelligent judgment of what the public interest demanded. And that is, above all, the safe and the saving policy for a President of the United States.

No Democrat with whom patriotism is not subordinated to private grudges will withhold his vote from Grover Cleveland. Of Republicans those who are entirely satisfied that Blaine and Logan faithfully represent the principles upon which the party that preserved the Union was founded will doubtless vote against him. Those of the Republican faith who are repelled by the most unwise choice made at Chicago last month will find no difficulty in voting for him, since he is one of the best representatives now to be found in public life of those administrative principles and reforms to which they are committed. A Democrat who has made enemies of the disreputable elements of his own party is not greatly to be feared by Republicans, even when he is a candidate for the presidency.

The *Times* will heartily support Governor Cleveland. In opposing Mr. Blaine it finds itself already upon impregnable ground and in excellent company. It has closely watched the career of the candidate nominated at Chicago yesterday, and it has entire confidence in his probity, in his intelligence, and in his administrative ability. He ought to be the next President of the United States, and we believe he will be.

The New York *Evening Post* said, later on: —

Of the kind of experience which the present situation in national affairs most imperatively calls for, experience in administration, Cleveland has more than any one who has entered the White House since 1860, more than any man whom either party has nominated within that period, except Seymour and Tilden — more than Lincoln, more than Garfield, more than Arthur. He laid at the start that best of all foundations for American statesmanship by becoming a good lawyer. He began his executive career by being a good county sheriff. He was next intrusted with the administration of a great city — as severe a test of a man's capacity in dealing with men and affairs as any American in our time can undergo. In both offices he gave boundless satisfaction to his fellow-citizens of both parties. His nomination for the governorship of this State came in due course, and at a crisis in State affairs which very closely resembled that which we are now witnessing in national affairs. His election by an unprecedented majority is now an old story. It was the beginning of a revolution. It was the first thorough fright the tricky and jobbing element in politics ever received here. It for the first time in their experience gave reform an air of reality. But it might, had Cleveland proved a weak or incompetent man, have turned out a very bad blow for pure politics.

Luckily he justified all the expectations and even all the hopes of those who voted for him. No friend of good government, who, in disregard of party ties, cast his vote for him, has had reason to regret it for one moment. He is in truth a Democrat of the better age of the Democratic party, when it was a party of simplicity and economy, and might almost have put its platform into the golden rule of giving every man his due, minding your own business, and asking nothing of government but light taxes and security in the field and by the fireside. No one who has entered the White House for half a century, except Lincoln in his second term, has offered such solid guarantees that as President he will do his own thinking and be his own master in the things which pertain to the Presidency.

At a meeting of the "Independents" in New York, July 22, 1884, the following remarks were made by George William Curtis: —

Upon the practical questions of tariff and finance, and other questions upon which both parties are divided within themselves, we also are divided in opinion. We shall vote therefore in the choice of representatives and other officers according to our individual opinions of their political views and their personal character. Divided on other questions, we are united in conviction that the fountain of office and honor should be pure, and that the highest office in the country should be filled by a man of absolutely unsuspected integrity. As there is no distinctive issue upon public policy presented for the consideration of the country, the character of the candidates becomes of the highest importance with all citizens who do not hold that party victory should be secured at any cost. While the Republican nomination presents a candidate whom we cannot support, the Democratic party presents one whose name is the synonym of political courage and honesty and of administrative reform. He has discharged every official trust with sole regard to the public welfare and with just disregard of mere partisan and personal advantage, which, with the applause and confidence of both parties, have raised him from the chief executive administration of a great city to that of a great State. His reserved, intelligent, and sincere support of reform in the civil service has firmly established that reform in the State and the cities of New York; and his personal convictions, proved by his official acts, more decisive than any possible platform declaration, are the guarantee that in its spirit and in its letter the reform would be enforced in the national administration. His high sense of duty, his absolute and unchallenged official integrity, his inflexible courage in resisting party pressure and public outcry, his great experience in the details of administration, and his commanding executive ability and independence, are precisely the qualities which the political situation demands in the chief executive officer of the government, to resist corporate monopoly on the one hand and demagogue communism on the other, and at home and abroad, without menace or fear, to protect every right of

American citizens, and to respect every right of friendly States by making political morality and private honesty the basis of constitutional administration. He is a Democrat who is happily free from all association with the fierce party differences of the slavery contest, and whose financial views are in harmony with those of the best men in both parties; and coming into public prominence at a time when official purity, courage, and character are of chief importance, he presents the qualities and the promise which independent voters desire, and which a great body of Republicans, believing those qualities to be absolutely indispensable in the administration of the government at this time, do not find in the candidate of their own party.

Such independent voters do not propose to ally themselves inextricably with any party. Such Republicans do not propose to abandon the Republican party nor to merge themselves in any other party, but they do propose to aid in defeating a Republican nomination which, not for reasons of expediency only, but for high moral and patriotic considerations, with a due regard for the Republican name and for the American character, was unfit to be made. They desire not to evade the proper responsibility of American citizens by declining to vote, and they desire also to make their votes as effective as possible for honest and pure and wise administration. How can such voters, who at this election cannot conscientiously support the Republican candidate, promote the objects which they desire to accomplish more surely than by supporting the candidate who represents the qualities, the spirit, and the purpose which they all agree in believing to be of controlling importance in this election? No citizen can rightfully avoid the issue or refuse to cast his vote. The ballot is a trust. Every voter is a trustee for good government, bound to answer to his private conscience for his public acts. This conference, therefore, assuming that Republicans and independent voters who for any reason, cannot sustain the Republican nomination desire to take the course which, under the necessary conditions and constitutional methods of a presidential election, will most readily and surely secure the result at which they aim, respectfully recommend to all such citizens to support the electors who will vote for Grover Cleveland, in order most effectually to enforce their conviction that nothing could more deeply stain the American name, and prove more disastrous to the public welfare, than the deliberate indifference of the people of the United States to increasing public corruption, and to the want of official integrity in the highest trusts of the government.

For the next three months this country was in the throes of a presidential election, James G. Blaine being the nominee of the Republican party. The result is well known. Grover Cleveland was elected President of the United States by a plurality of the popular vote of 69,806. He received 219 electoral votes, against 182 cast for Mr. Blaine. This result was received with much gratification by the entire nation, and public opinion, when expressed without partisan bias, is a unit as to the solid advantages to this country derived from the election of Grover Cleveland. One question of importance was soon settled by Mr. Cleveland.

After the election in December, 1884, the National Civil Service Reform League addressed a letter to the President, intended to draw from him more explicitly a statement of his views in regard to civil service reform. To this Mr. Cleveland returned a reply, dated December 25, in which he declared himself pledged to a "fair and honest enforcement" of the civil service law, both because of his "conception of true Democratic faith and public duty," which required "that this and all other statutes should be in good faith and without evasion enforced." But he added a voluntary promise to enlarge and extend the scope and operation of the actual statute, as follows : —

"There is a class of government positions which

are not within the letter of the civil service statute, but which are so disconnected with the policy of an administration that the removal therefrom of present incumbents, in my opinion, should not be made during the terms for which they were appointed solely on partisan grounds, and for the purpose of putting in their places those who are in political accord with the appointing power. But many now holding such positions have forfeited all just claim to retention, because they have used their places for party purposes, in disregard of their duty to the people, and because, instead of being decent public servants, they have proved themselves offensive partisans and unscrupulous manipulators of local party management. The lessons of the past should be unlearned, and such officials, as well as their successors, should be taught that efficiency, fitness, and devotion to public duty are the conditions of their continuance in public place, and that the quiet and unobtrusive exercise of individual political rights is the reasonable measure of their party service."

In April, 1885, Mr. Cleveland highly gratified the true friends of civil service reform by appointing Henry G. Pearson, the Republican incumbent, for a full term as postmaster of New York. This appointment in the public interest was made in the face of a party pressure and a party denunciation which few men would have had the strength to resist, and the act was regarded not only as a proof of Mr. Cleveland's firmness and courage, but as a guarantee that he would adhere to his civil service reform pledges.

Prior to the election of Cleveland there were

many phases of public opinion as to his views in relation to civil service, and, as his election was largely due to the unanimity of the Independent party in casting their votes with the Democrats, it is perhaps as well to give here the reasons which brought this about, as presented by Carl Schurz, a prominent Independent.

SPEECH OF HON. CARL SCHURZ BEFORE THE MEETING OF INDEPENDENT VOTERS, BROOKLYN, AUGUST 5, 1884.

... The Democratic party has never presented a candidate whom any friend of good government, Democrat or Republican, could see step into the presidential chair with a greater feeling of security than Grover Cleveland. This time, therefore, is uncommonly propitious for a change of power, on account of the safety with which it can be effected. ...

Mr. Blaine's advocates loudly complain that Governor Cleveland is not a statesman. It must be admitted that he is not a statesman in the Blaine sense. If he were, it would be dangerous to vote for him. He has evidently not the genius to be all things to everybody. He is not magnetic enough to draw every rascal to his support. He will probably be cold enough to freeze every job out of the White House. He is not brilliant enough to cover the whole world with flighty schemes. But, unless I am much mistaken, he possesses very much of that kind of statesmanship which is now especially required, and for which Mr. Blaine has conspicuously disqualified himself. And that is the statesmanship of honest and efficient administration. What is the kind of business which under present circumstances the executive branch of the national government has to attend to? It is in the main administrative business. It is to see to it that the laws be faithfully and efficiently executed, and, to that end, to introduce and maintain honest and efficient methods for the execution of the laws, and to enforce the necessary responsibility. This is administration, and this is under present circumstances the principal business of the executive. No flighty genius, therefore, is required to *make* business for the government; but what we want is solid ability and courageous integrity to see to it that the business which is found there be well done.

Of this kind of statesmanship Mr. Cleveland, as all who have impartially observed his career will admit, possesses in a high degree the instinct, and now also the experience. When he entered upon his duties as mayor of Buffalo, a few years ago, he said, " It seems to me that a successful and faithful ministration of the government of a city may be accomplished by constantly bearing in mind that we are the trustees and agents of our fellow-citizens, holding their funds in sacred trust to be expended for their benefit; that we should at all times be prepared to render an honest account to them touching the manner of its expenditure; and that the affairs of the city should be conducted as far as possible upon the same principles as a good business man manages his private concerns." You may say that this is neither very brilliant nor quite original. But it contains after all the fundamental principles of honest and efficient administration, applicable not only to a city, but to a State and to the nation. And when a public man coming into power speaks such words, and fully understands what they mean, and has the ability and courage to give them full effect, he possesses a statesmanship for executive office infinitely more valuable to the country than Mr. Blaine's statesmanlike skill and experience in making himself "useful in various channels," and being a deadhead in none.

And that Mr. Cleveland did understand the meaning of what he said, and was determined to carry it out, he showed sometimes in a way which astonished the natives. Here is an instance: When the city council of Buffalo, composed of Democrats and Republicans, had passed a resolution approving an extravagant contract for street-cleaning, his veto message contained the following language: " This is a time for plain speech. I withhold my assent from the same [the resolution] because I regard it as the culmination of a most barefaced, impudent, and shameless scheme to betray the interests of the people and to worse than squander the public money. I will not be misunderstood in this matter. There are those whose votes were given for this resolution whom I cannot and will not suspect of a wilful neglect of the interests they are sworn to protect; but it has been fully demonstrated that there are influences, both in and about your honorable body, which it behooves every honest man to watch and avoid with the greatest care." This meant as plainly as parliamentary language could express it: "Gentlemen, there are some scoundrels among you. I know it. And I want you to know that I know it, and that I watch you, and that your schemes will not succeed as long as I am here." I like that kind of statesmanship. The taxpayers of Buffalo liked it. The people of the State soon showed that they liked it. And I think the people of the United States would like it too, the knaves always excepted.

Mr. Cleveland had never been a professed civil service reformer. But he soon showed that he understood and adopted the vital principles of civil service reform by instinct. He said in his letter of acceptance, when nominated for the governorship, "Subordinates in public place should be selected and retained for their efficiency, and not because they may be used to accomplish partisan ends. The people have a right to demand here, as in cases of private employment, that their money be paid to those who will render the best service in return, and that the appointment to and tenure of such places should depend upon ability and merit." This is the whole in a nutshell. And he not only understood it and said it, but he acted accordingly when in power, for he favored and signed and faithfully helped to execute the Civil Service Act for the State of New York, which embodies just these principles, although he knew that it cut off the loaves and fishes of public spoil in a great measure from his own party. But more. He said in the same letter of acceptance, "The expenditure of money to influence the action of the people at the polls, or to secure legislation, is calculated to excite the gravest concern. It is useless and foolish to shut our eyes to the fact that this evil exists among us, and the party which leads in an honest effort to return to better and purer methods will receive the confidence of our citizens and secure their support." Having said this, he favored and signed a prohibition of political assessments in the civil service of New York, although he knew that this measure would most severely curtail the electioneering funds of his own party.

As a member of the Civil Service Reform Association, I may say that, when we prepared and urged a legislative reform measure, we never inquired whether Governor Cleveland, although a Democrat, would sign it, because we knew he would if it was a good one. When the citizens of New York City sought to correct the crying abuses of their municipal government, they, too, always counted with the same confidence upon the Governor, no matter whether the Democratic or the Republican party might be hurt by a measure of true reform, and that confidence was always justified. And, by the way, it is rather a shabby piece of business that some of the gentlemen who leaned upon the Governor as one of their principal pillars of strength, and were then full of praise of him for his courageous resistance to party pressure, should throw paltry quibbles at him since he has become a candidate for the Presidency. Had he not been nominated, it would have been said that the unbending courage for the right with which he resisted pressure coming from his own party was the very thing that defeated him. It was, indeed, the thing which made his enemies hate him so bitterly. But take his whole record. When he ceased to be mayor of Buffalo, a Republican paper said, "Yesterday Buffalo lost the best mayor she ever had." When he ceases to be Governor, to become President of the United States, these very gentlemen will say, "New York never had a more efficient Governor than this."

Mr. Cleveland resigned his office as Governor of the State of New York upon the meeting of the State Legislature, January 6, 1885, but continued his residence in Albany. The intervening period between his resignation as Governor and his inauguration as President was occupied in receiving visits from many of the leading men of the Democratic party. On February 27, 1885, a letter of Mr. Cleveland was published in reply to one signed by several members of Congress. In this letter he indicated his opposition to an increased coinage of silver, and suggested a *suspension* of the purchase and coinage of that metal as a measure of safety, in order to prevent a financial crisis and the ultimate expulsion of gold and silver. His inaugural address was written during the ten days previous to his departure for Washington. On the evening of

March 2, 1885, Grover Cleveland quietly left Albany, accompanied by his two sisters, Daniel Manning, and Colonel Daniel S. Lamont, arriving in Washington at 7 A. M. On the following day he went to the Capitol with President Arthur, and, after the usual preliminaries had been completed, he delivered his inaugural address from the steps of the Capitol, on March 4, 1885, as follows: —

INAUGURAL ADDRESS.

FELLOW-CITIZENS, — In the presence of this vast assemblage of my countrymen I am about to supplement, and seal by the oath which I shall take, the manifestation of the will of a great and free people. In the exercise of their power, and the right of self-government, they have committed to one of their fellow-citizens a supreme and sacred trust, and he here consecrates himself to their service. This impressive ceremony adds little to the solemn sense of responsibility with which I contemplate the duty I owe to all the people of the land. Nothing can relieve me from anxiety lest by any act of mine their interests may suffer, and nothing is needed to strengthen my resolution to engage every faculty and effort in the promotion of their welfare.

Amid the din of party strife, the people's choice was made, but its attendant circumstances have demonstrated anew the strength and safety of a government by the people. In each succeeding year it more clearly appears that our democratic principle needs no apology, and that in its fearless and faithful application is to be found the surest guarantee of good government. But the best results in the operation of a government wherein every citizen has a share largely depend upon a proper limitation of purely partisan zeal and effort, and a correct appreciation of the time when the heat of the partisan should be merged in the patriotism of the citizen.

To-day the executive branch of the government is transferred to new keeping. But this is still the government of all the people, and it should be none the less an object of their affectionate solicitude. At this hour the animosities of political strife, the bitterness of partisan defeat, and the exultation of partisan triumph, should be supplanted by an ungrudging acquiescence in the popular will, and a sober conscientious concern for the general weal. Moreover, if from this hour we cheerfully and honestly abandon all sectional prejudice and distrust, and determine, with manly confidence in one another, to work out harmoniously the achievements of our national destiny, we shall deserve to realize all the benefits which our happy form of government can bestow.

On this auspicious occasion we may well renew the pledge of our devotion to the Constitution, which, launched by the founders of the republic and consecrated by their prayers and patriotic devotion, has for almost a century borne the hopes and aspirations of a great people through prosperity and peace, and through the shock of foreign conflicts and the perils of domestic strife and vicissitudes. By the father of his country our Constitution was commended for adoption, as "the result of a spirit of amity and mutual concession." In that same spirit it should be administered, in order to promote the lasting welfare of the country, and to secure the full measure of its priceless benefits to us and to those who will succeed to the blessings of our national life. The large variety of diverse and competing interests subject to federal control, persistently seeking the recognition of their claims, need give us no fear that "the greatest good to the greatest number" will fail to be accomplished if in the halls of national legislation that spirit of amity and mutual concession shall prevail in which the Constitution had its birth. If this involves the surrender or postponement of private interests, and the abandonment of local advantages, compensation will be found in the assurance that thus the common interest is subserved and the general welfare advanced.

In the discharge of my official duty I shall endeavor to be guided by a just and unstrained construction of the Constitution, a careful observance of the distinction between the powers granted to the federal government and those reserved to the State or to the people, and by a cautious appreciation of those functions which by the Constitution and laws have been especially assigned to the executive branch of the government. But he who takes the oath to-day to preserve, protect, and defend the Constitution of the United States only assumes the solemn obligation which every patriotic citizen — on the farm, in the workshop, in the busy marts of trade, and everywhere — should share with him. The Constitution which prescribes his oath, my countrymen, is yours, the government you have chosen him to administer for a time is yours, the suffrage which executes the will of freemen is yours, the laws and the entire scheme of our civil rule — from the town meeting to the State capitol and the national capitol — is yours. Your every voter, as surely as your chief magistrate, — under the same high sanction, though in a different sphere, — exercises a public trust. Nor is this all. Every citizen owes to the country a vigilant watch and close scrutiny of its public servants, and a fair and reasonable estimate of their fidelity and usefulness. Thus is the people's will impressed upon the whole framework of our civil polity, — municipal, State, and federal, — and this is the price of our liberty and the inspiration of our faith in the republic. It is the duty of those serving the people in public place to closely limit public expenditures to the actual needs of the government, economically administered, because this bounds the right of the government to exact tribute from the earnings of labor or the property of the citizen, and because public extravagance begets extravagance among the people. We should never be ashamed of the simplicity and prudential economies which are best suited to the operation of a republican form of government and most compatible with the mission of the American people. Those who are selected for a limited time to manage public affairs are still of the people, and may do much by their example to encourage, consistently with the dignity of their official functions, that plain way of life which among their fellow-citizens aids integrity and promotes thrift and prosperity.

FOREIGN POLICY.

The genius of our institutions, the needs of our people in their home life, and the attention which is demanded for the settlement and development of the resources of our vast territory, dictate the scrupulous avoidance of any departure from that foreign policy commended by the history, the traditions, and the prosperity of our republic. It is the policy of independence favored by our position and defended by our known love of justice and by our power. It is the policy of peace suitable to our interests. It is the policy of neutrality, rejecting any share in foreign broils and ambitions upon other continents, and repelling their intrusion here. It is the policy of Monroe and of Washington and Jefferson — " Peace, commerce, and honest friendship with all nations; entangling alliance with none."

FINANCIAL POLICY.

A due regard for the interests and prosperity of all the people demands that our finances shall be established upon such a sound and sensible basis as will secure the safety and confidence of business interests, and make the wage of labor sure and steady, and that our system of revenue shall be so adjusted as to relieve the people of unnecessary taxation, having a due regard to the interests of capital invested and workingmen employed in American industries, and preventing the accumulation of a surplus in the treasury to tempt extravagance and waste. Care for the property of the nation and for the needs of future settlers requires that the public domain should be protected from purloining schemes and unlawful occupation.

INDIAN POLICY.

The convenience of the people demands that the Indians within our boundaries shall be fairly and honestly treated as wards of the government, and their education and civilization promoted with a view to their ultimate citizenship, and that polygamy in the Territories, destructive of the family relations and offensive to the moral sense of the civilized world, shall be repressed. The laws should be rigidly enforced which prohibit the immigration of a servile class to compete with American labor, with no intention of acquiring citizenship, and bringing with them and retaining habits and customs repugnant to our civilization.

CIVIL SERVICE REFORM.

The people demand reform in the administration of the government, and the application of business principles to public affairs. As a means to this end, civil service reform should be in good faith enforced. Our citizens have the right to protection from the incompetency of public employés, who hold their places solely as the reward of partisan service, and from the corrupting influence of those who promise and the vicious methods of those who expect such rewards. And those who worthily seek public employment have the right to insist that merit and competency shall be recognized, instead of party subserviency or the surrender of honest political belief.

THE FREEDMEN.

In the administration of a government pledged to do equal and exact justice to all men there should be no pretext for anxiety touching the protection of the freedmen in their rights or their security in the enjoyment of their privileges under the Constitution and its amendments. All discussion as to their fitness for the place accorded to them as American citizens is idle and unprofitable except as it suggests the necessity for their improvement. The fact that they are citizens entitles them to all the rights due to that relation, and charges them with all its duties, obligations, and responsibilities.

CLOSING REMARKS.

These topics and the constant and ever varying wants of an active and enterprising population may well receive the attention and the patriotic endeavors of all who make and execute the federal law. Our duties are practical, and call for industrious application, an intelligent perception of the claims for public office, and, above all, a firm determination by united action to secure to all the people of the land the full benefits of the best form of government ever vouchsafed to man. And let us not trust to human effort alone, but, humbly acknowledging the power and goodness of Almighty God, who presides over the destiny of nations, and who has at all times been revealed in our country's history, let us invoke his aid and his blessing upon our labors.

This admirable presentation of the views of Grover Cleveland was accepted by the people of the United States as his programme for their government, and the result of his administration has been unanimously admitted to be full evidence of the wisdom of his judgment and his honest intentions to do all in his power to carry out the views thus presented. On the 13th of March he issued a proclamation in reference to the removal of unlawful white intruders from Oklahoma, Indian Territory. He ordered a naval expedition for the protection of American citizens at Aspinwall. By his instruction General Sheridan visited the Indian Territory to report upon the condition of the various tribes who were threatening war with each other. In the interest of the great agricultural population of the West, on the 10th of August, 1885, the President issued an order warning all cattle-graziers to remove all fences. On the 8th of December, 1885, Grover Cleveland issued his first message to Congress, at the beginning of the first session of the Forty-ninth Congress. We have only room for some of the special matters referred to by the President. Our relations with foreign nations were all friendly. The attention of Congress was specially called to the importance of our diplomatic and consular service, with suggestions for its improvement; also to the prohibitory duties upon paintings by foreign artists, with a recommendation that they should be abolished.

OUR REVENUES.

The fact that our revenues are in excess of the actual needs of an economical administration of the government justifies a reduction in the amount exacted from the people for its support. Our government is but the means established by the will of a free people, by which certain principles are applied which they have adopted for their benefit and protection; and it is never better administered, and its true spirit is never better observed, than when the people's taxation for its support is scrupulously limited to the actual necessity of expenditure, and distributed according to a just and equitable plan.

The proposition with which we have to deal is the reduction of the revenue received by the government and indirectly paid by the people from customs duties. The question of free trade is not involved, nor is there now any occasion for the general discussion of the wisdom or expediency of a protective system.

Justice and fairness dictate that, in any modification of our present laws relating to revenue, the industries and interests which have been encouraged by such laws, and in which our citizens have large investments, should not be ruthlessly injured or destroyed. We should also deal with the subject in such manner as to protect the interests of American labor, which is the capital of our workingmen; its stability and proper remuneration furnish the most justifiable pretext for a protective policy.

Within these limitations a certain reduction should be made in our customs revenue. The amount of such reduction having been determined, the inquiry follows, where can it best be remitted, and what articles can best be released from duty, in the interest of our citizens?

I think the reduction should be made in the revenue derived from a tax upon the imported necessaries of life. We thus directly lessen the cost of living in every family of the land, and release to the people in every humble home a larger measure of the rewards of frugal industry.

OUR NAVY.

All must admit the importance of an effective navy to a nation like ours, having such an extended seacoast to protect. And yet we have not a single vessel of war that could keep the seas against a first-class vessel of any important power. Such a condition ought not longer to continue. The nation that cannot resist aggression is constantly exposed to it. Its foreign policy is of necessity weak, and its negotiations are conducted with disadvantage, because it is not in condition to enforce the terms dictated by its sense of right and justice.

Inspired, as I am, by the hope, shared by all patriotic citizens, that the day is not very far distant when our navy will be such as befits our standing among the nations of the earth, and rejoiced at every step that leads in the direction of such a consummation, I deem it my duty to especially direct the attention of Congress to the close of the report of the Secretary of the Navy, in which the humiliating weakness of the present organization of his department is exhibited, and the startling abuses and waste of its present methods are exposed. The conviction is forced upon us, with the certainty of mathematical demonstration, that, before we proced further in the restoration of a navy, we need a thoroughly reorganized Navy Department. The fact that within seventeen years more than seventy-five millions of dollars have been spent in the construction, repair, equipment, and armament of vessels, and the further fact that, instead of an effective and creditable fleet, we have only the discontent and apprehension of a nation undefended by war vessels, added to the disclosures now made, do not permit us to doubt that every attempt to revive our navy has thus far, for the most part, been misdirected, and all our efforts in that direction have been little better than blind gropings and expensive, aimless follies.

Unquestionably, if we are content with the maintenance of a Navy Department simply as a shabby ornament to the government, a constant watchfulness may prevent some of the scandal and abuse which have found their way into our present organization, and its incurable waste may be reduced to the minimum. But if we desire to build ships for present usefulness, instead of naval reminders of the days that are past, we must have a department organized for the work, supplied with all the talent and ingenuity our country affords, prepared to take advantage of the experience of other nations, systematized so that all effort shall unite and lead in one direction, and fully imbued with the conviction that war vessels, though new, are useless unless they combine all that the ingenuity of man has up to this day brought forth relating to their construction.

I earnestly commend the portion of the secretary's report devoted to this subject to the attention of Congress, in the hope that his suggestions touching the reorganization of his department may be adopted as the first step toward the reconstruction of our navy.

OUR INDIANS.

They are within the care of our government, and their rights are, or should be, protected from invasion by the most solemn obligations. They are properly enough called the wards of the government; and it should be borne in mind that this guardianship involves, on our part, efforts for the improvement of their condition and the enforcement of their rights. There seems to be general concurrence in the proposition that the ultimate object of their treatment should be their civilization and citizenship. Fitted by these to keep pace in the march of progress with the advanced civilization about them, they will readily assimilate with the mass of our population, assuming the responsibilities and receiving the protection incident to this condition.

OUR LANDS.

It is not for the "common benefit of the United States" that a large area of the public lands should be acquired, directly or through fraud, in the hands of a single individual. The nation's strength is in the people. The nation's prosperity is in their prosperity. The nation's glory is in the equality of her justice. The nation's perpetuity is in the patriotism of all her people. Hence, as far as practicable, the plan adopted in the disposal of the public lands should have in view the original policy, which encouraged many purchasers of these lands for homes, and discouraged the massing of large areas. Exclusive of Alaska, about three-fifths of the national domain has been sold, or subjected to contract or grant. Of the remaining two-fifths, a considerable portion is either mountain or desert. A rapidly increasing population creates a growing demand for homes, and the accumulation of wealth inspires an eager competition to obtain the public land for speculative purposes. In the future, this collision of interests will be more marked than in the past, and the execution of the nation's trust, in behalf of our settlers, will be more difficult. I therefore commend to your attention the recommendations contained in the report of the Secretary of the Interior with reference to the repeal and modification of certain of our land laws.

OUR SOLDIERS.

While there is no expenditure of the public funds which the people more cheerfully approve than that made in recognition of the services of our soldiers, living and dead, the sentiment underlying the subject should not be vitiated by the introduction of any fraudulent practices. Therefore it is fully as important that the rolls should be cleansed of all those who by fraud have secured a place thereon as that meritorious claims should be speedily examined and adjusted. The reforms in the methods of doing the business of this bureau which have lately been inaugurated promise better results in both these directions.

OUR HOMES.

The strength, the perpetuity, and the destiny of the nation rest upon our homes, established by the law of God, guarded by parental care, regulated by parental authority, and sanctified by parental love.

These are not the homes of polygamy.

The mothers of our land, who rule the nation as they mould the characters and guide the actions of their sons, live according to God's holy ordinances, and each, secure and happy in the exclusive love of the father of her children, sheds the warm light of true womanhood, unperverted and unpolluted, upon all within her pure and wholesome family circle.

These are not the cheerless, crushed, and unwomanly mothers of polygamy.

The fathers of our families are the best citizens of the republic. Wife and children are the sources of patriotism, and conjugal and parental affection beget devotion to the country. The man who, undefiled with plural marriage, is surrounded in his single home with his wife and children has a stake in the country which inspires him with respect for its laws and courage for its defence.

These are not the fathers of polygamous families.

There is no feature of this practice, or the system which sanctions it, which is not opposed to all that is of value in our institutions.

There should be no relaxation in the firm but just execution of the law now in operation, and I should be glad to approve such further discreet legislation as will rid the country of this blot upon its fair fame.

Since the people upholding polygamy in our Territories are reënforced by immigration from other lands, I recommend that a law be passed to prevent the importation of Mormons into the country. . . .

OUR FARMERS.

The agricultural interest of the country demands just recognition and liberal encouragement. It sustains with certainty and unfailing strength our nation's prosperity by the products of its steady toil, and bears its full share of the burden of taxation without complaint. Our agriculturists have but slight personal representation in the councils of the nation, and are generally content with the humbler duties of citizenship, and willing to trust to the bounty of nature for a reward of their labor. But the magnitude and value of this industry is appreciated when the statement is made that of our total annual exports more than three-fourths are the products of agriculture, and of our total population nearly one-half are exclusively engaged in that occupation. . . .

CIVIL SERVICE REFORM.

I am inclined to think that there is no sentiment more general in the minds of the people of our country than a conviction of the correctness of the principle upon which the law enforcing civil service reform is based. In its present condition, the law regulates only a part of the subordinate public positions throughout the country. It applies the test of fitness to applicants for these places by means of a competitive examination, and gives large discretion to the commissioners as to the character of the examination, and many other matters connected with its execution. Thus the rules and regulations adopted by the commission have much to do with the practical usefulness of the statute, and with the results of its application.

The people may well trust the commission to execute the law with perfect fairness and with as little irritation as is possible. But of course no relaxation of the principle which underlies it, and no weakening of the safeguards which surround it, can be expected. Experience in its administration will probably suggest amendment of the methods of its execution, but I venture to hope that we shall never again be remitted to the system which distributes public positions purely as rewards for partisan service. Doubts may well be entertained whether our government could survive the strain of a continuance of this system, which, upon every change of administration, inspires an immense army of claimants for office to lay siege to the patronage of government, engrossing the time of public officers with their importunities, spreading abroad the contagion of their disappointment, and filling the air with the tumult of their discontent. . . .

CONCLUSION.

In conclusion, I commend to the wise care and thoughtful attention of Congress the needs, the welfare, and the aspirations of an intelligent and generous nation. To subordinate these to the narrow advantages of partisanship or the accomplishment of selfish aims is to violate the people's trust and betray the people's interests. But an individual sense of responsibility on the part of each of us, and a stern determination to perform our duty well, must give us place among those who have added in their day and generation to the glory and prosperity of our beloved land.

GROVER CLEVELAND.

WASHINGTON, December 8, 1885.

It will thus be seen that the President kept constantly in view all the points suggested in his inaugural address, and a perusal of this work will indicate, beyond contradiction, a consistent following out of his own convictions as to what was best for the interests of the nation. On June 2, 1886, Grover Cleveland was married to Frances Folsom. It is eminently right and proper that some allusion should be made to an event which has added so much to the power of the executive. While the President has secured to himself the esteem and admiration of his fellow-citizens for his thoroughly honest and common-sense policy of administrating the affairs of the nation, Mrs. Cleveland has secured our hearts; in her presence partisanship is at an end, and there is but one unanimous feeling of love and affection for her, from one extreme of this great land to the other. On the 6th of December, 1886, the President delivered his second annual message to Congress, and from the tenor of the following selections it will be seen that his persistence in the plans promulgated in his inaugural had already produced good results.

OUR FOREIGN POLICY.

Our government has consistently maintained its relations of friendship toward all other powers, and of neighborly interest toward those whose possessions are contiguous to our own. Few questions have arisen during the past year with other governments, and none of those are beyond the reach of settlement in friendly counsel. . . .

Cases have continued to occur in Germany, giving rise to much correspondence in relation to the privilege of sojourn of our naturalized citizens of German origin revisiting the land of their birth, yet I am happy to state that our relations with that country have lost none of their accustomed cordiality. . . .

A treaty of extradition between the United States and Japan, the first concluded by that empire, has been lately proclaimed. . . .

The encouraging development of beneficial and intimate relations between the United States and Mexico, which has been so marked within the past few years, is at once the occasion of congratulation and of friendly solicitude. I urgently renew my former representation of the need of speedy legislation by Congress to carry into effect the Reciprocity Commercial Convention of January 20, 1883.

Our commercial treaty of 1831 with Mexico was terminated, according to its provisions in 1881, upon notification given by Mexico, in pursuance of her announced policy of recasting all her commercial treaties. Mexico has since concluded with several foreign governments new treaties of commerce and navigation, defining alien rights of trade, property, and residence, treatment of shipping, consular privileges, and the like. Our yet unexecuted Reciprocity Convention of 1883 covers none of these points, the settlement of which is so necessary to good relationship. I propose to initiate with Mexico negotiations for a new and enlarged treaty of commerce and navigation. . . .

OUR CONSULAR SERVICE.

Pursuant to a provision of the diplomatic and consular appropriation act, approved July 1, 1886, the estimates submitted by the Secretary of State for the maintenance of the consular service have been recast, on the basis of salaries for all officers to whom such allowance is deemed advisable. Advantage has been taken of this to redistribute the salaries of the offices now appropriated for, in accordance with the work performed, the importance of the representative duties of the incumbent, and the cost of living at each post. The last consideration has been too often lost sight of in the allowances heretofore made. The compensation which may suffice for the decent maintenance of a worthy and capable officer in a position of onerous and representative trust at a post readily accessible, and where the necessaries of life are abundant and cheap, may prove an inadequate pittance in distant lands, where the better part of a year's pay is consumed in reaching the post of duty, and where the comforts of ordinary civilized existence can only be obtained with difficulty and at exorbitant cost. I trust that, in considering the submitted schedules, no mistaken theory of economy will perpetuate a system which in the past has virtually closed to deserving talent many offices where capacity and attainments of a high order are indispensable, and in not a few instances has brought discredit on our national character, and entailed embarrassment and even suffering on those deputed to uphold our dignity and interests abroad.

In connection with this subject, I earnestly reiterate the practical necessity of supplying some mode of trustworthy inspection and report of the manner in which the consulates are conducted. In the absence of such reliable information, efficiency can scarcely be rewarded, or its opposite corrected. . . .

OUR REVENUES.

In my last annual message to Congress, attention was directed to the fact that the revenues of the government exceeded its actual needs; and it was suggested that legislative action should be taken to relieve the people from the unnecessary burden of taxation thus made apparent.

In view of the pressing importance of the subject, I deem it my duty to again urge its consideration. . . .

In readjusting the burdens of federal taxation, a sound public policy requires that such of our citizens as have built up large and important industries under present conditions should not be suddenly and to their injury deprived of advantages to which they have adapted their business; but, if the public good requires it, they should be content with such consideration as shall deal fairly and cautiously with their interests, while the just demand of the people for relief from needless taxation is honestly answered.

A reasonable and timely submission to such a demand should certainly be possible without disastrous shock to any interest; and a cheerful concession sometimes averts abrupt and heedless action, often the outgrowth of impatience and delayed justice.

THE LABOR QUESTION.

Due regard should be also accorded, in any proposed readjustment, to the interests of American labor so far as they are involved. We congratulate ourselves that there is among us no laboring class, fixed within unyielding bounds and doomed under all conditions to the inexorable fate of daily toil. We recognize in labor a chief factor in the wealth of the republic, and we treat those who have it in their keeping as citizens entitled to the most careful regard and thoughtful attention. This regard and attention should be awarded them not only because labor is the capital of our workingmen, justly entitled to its share of government favor, but for the further and not less important reason that the laboring man surrounded by his family in his humble home, as a consumer, is vitally interested in all that cheapens the cost of living and enables him to bring within his domestic circle additional comforts and advantages.

This relation of the workingman to the revenue laws of the

country, and the manner in which it palpably influences the question of wages, should not be forgotten in the justifiable prominence given to the proper maintenance of the supply and protection of well paid labor. And these considerations suggest such an arrangement of government revenues as shall reduce the expense of living, while it does not curtail the opportunity for work or reduce the compensation of American labor, and injuriously affect its condition and the dignified place it holds in the estimation of our people. . . .

I recommend that, keeping in view all these considerations, the increasing and unnecessary surplus of national income annually accumulating be released to the people, by an amendment to our revenue laws, which shall cheapen the price of the necessaries of life and give freer entrance to such imported materials as by American labor may be manufactured into marketable commodities.

Nothing can be accomplished, however, in the direction of this much needed reform, unless the subject is approached in a patriotic spirit of devotion to the interests of the entire country and with a willingness to yield something for the public good. . . .

OUR FORTIFICATIONS.

The defenceless condition of our seacoast and lake frontier is perfectly palpable; the examinations made must convince us all that certain of our cities, named in the report of the board, should be fortified, and that work on the most important of these fortifications should be commenced at once; the work has been thoroughly considered and laid out, the Secretary of War reports, but all is delayed in default of Congressional action. . . .

OUR INDIANS.

The exhibit made of the condition of our Indian population and the progress of the work for their enlightenment, notwithstanding the many embarrassments which hinder the better administration of this important branch of the service, is a gratifying and hopeful one. . . .

There is less opposition to the education and training of the Indian youth, as shown by the increased attendance upon the schools, and there is a yielding tendency for the individual holding of lands. Development and advancement in these directions are essential, and should have every encouragement. As the rising generation are taught the language of civilization and trained in habits of industry, they should assume the duties, privileges, and responsibilities of citizenship.

No obstacle should hinder the location and settlement of any Indian willing to take land in severalty; on the contrary, the inclination to do so should be stimulated at all times when proper and expedient. But there is no authority of law for making allotments on some of the reservations, and on others the allotments provided for are so small that the Indians, though ready and desiring to settle down, are not willing to accept such small areas, when their reservations contain ample lands to afford them homesteads of sufficient size to meet their present and future needs. . . .

OUR SOLDIERS.

The American people, with a patriotic and grateful regard for our ex-soldiers,— too broad and too sacred to be monopolized by any special advocates,— are not only willing but anxious that equal and exact justice should be done to all honest claimants for pensions. In their sight the friendless and destitute soldier, dependent on public charity, if otherwise entitled, has precisely the same right to share in the provision made for those who fought their country's battles as those better able, through friends and influence, to push their claims. Every pension that is granted under our present plan upon any other grounds than actual service and injury or disease incurred in such service, and every instance of the many in which pensions are increased on other grounds than the merits of the claim, work an injustice to the brave and crippled, but poor and friendless soldier who is entirely neglected or who must be content with the smallest sum allowed under general laws. . . .

CIVIL SERVICE REFORM.

The continued operation of the law relating to our civil service has added the most convincing proofs of its necessity and usefulness. It is a fact worthy of note that every public officer who has a just idea of his duty to the people testifies to the value of this reform. Its staunchest friends are found among those who understand it best, and its warmest supporters are those who are restrained and protected by its requirements.

The meaning of such restraint and protection is not appreciated by those who want places under the government, regardless of merit and efficiency, nor by those who insist that the selection for such places should rest upon a proper credential showing active partisan work. They mean to public officers, if not their lives, the only opportunity afforded them to attend to public business, and they mean to the good people of the country the better performance of the work of their government.

It is exceedingly strange that the scope and nature of this reform are so little understood, and that so many things not included within its plan are called by its name. When cavil yields more fully to examination, the system will have large additions to the number of its friends.

Our civil service reform may be imperfect in some of its details; it may be misunderstood and opposed; it may not always be faithfully applied; its designs may sometimes miscarry through mistake or wilful intent; it may sometimes tremble under the assaults of its enemies or languish under the misguided zeal of impractical friends; but if the people of this country ever submit to the banishment of its underlying principle from the operation of their government, they will abandon the surest guarantee of the safety and success of American institutions. . . .

CONCLUSION.

In conclusion, I earnestly invoke such wise action on the part of the people's legislators as will subserve the public good and demonstrate during the remaining days of the Congress as at present organized its ability and inclination to so meet the people's needs that it shall be gratefully remembered by an expectant constituency.   GROVER CLEVELAND.

WASHINGTON, December 6, 1886.

We have in the preceding pages attempted to give some account of the man in whose hands are held to a large extent the welfare of this nation. We have shown that from his early life, and through his occupation of the offices of mayor, Governor, and President, he has been thoroughly consistent. While holding the latter high position, he has simply amplified, in carrying out, the same rules of government which he set forth as mayor and Governor. In all his messages there is the same clear ring: We, the officers of the government of the United States, are placed in power for the good of our country; let the result of our administration prove to the world our ability as Democrats to secure the best welfare of our fellow-citizens in our management of the great trust committed to our charge. Mr. Cleveland's great popularity is largely due to the fact that he is always perfectly candid. He impresses the people as a truthful, practical man, who devotes himself conscientiously to the discharge of his duties; also as a man of moral courage, who when he believes it is right and just to veto an obnoxious bill does not hesitate to do it. All these facts have led to the *unanimous* renomination of Grover Cleveland by the Democratic party, an incident without precedent in the history of the country. The principle which he represents is the honest conduct of the public business, and that principle has been conscientiously carried out through the administration now drawing to a close, so far as the position of the President has permitted him to act. The record of this administration is open to the people, and, so far as possible in the space allotted, we have endeavored to show that the President has been thoroughly supported by a cabinet in whose official position there has been but little change during his administration.

CHAPTER V.

THE STATE DEPARTMENT.

All correspondence with the public ministers and consuls of the United States, all correspondence with the representatives of foreign powers accredited to the United States, and negotiations relating to the foreign affairs of the United States, must pass through the hands of the Secretary of State. He is also the medium of correspondence between the President and the chief executive of the several States of the United States. To him is confided the custody of the great seal of the United States, and he countersigns and affixes such seal to all executive proclamations, to commissions, and to warrants for pardon and the extradition of fugitives from justice. He stands first in rank among the members of the Cabinet. He is, beside, the custodian of the treaties made with foreign States and of the laws of the United States. It is his privilege to grant and issue passports, and exequaturs to foreign consuls in the United States. He publishes the laws and resolutions of Congress, amendments to the Constitution, and proclamations declaring the admission of new States into the Union. It is further his duty to publish certain annual reports to Congress relating to commercial information received from diplomatic and consular officers of the United States. Indeed, his position in the Cabinet is very important and responsible.

THE SECRETARY OF STATE.

Thomas F. Bayard

creditably and honorably fills the high post of Secretary of Sate.

The Bayard family have been residents in this country for over two hundred years, and trace their descent from the same family as that of Chevalier Bayard, the knight "sans peur et sans reproche." Peter Bayard, the direct ancestor of the Secretary of State, settled in what is now known as the State of Maryland, where he purchased some 25,000 acres. John Bayard, grandson of Peter, took an active part in the Revolutionary war, serving as colonel of cavalry. The historian Bancroft refers to him as "a patriot of singular purity of character and disinterestedness." He was later a member of the Continental Congress.

Richard Bassett, the great grandfather of our present Secretary of State, was an active patriot of the Revolution, and was a delegate to the convention that framed the Federal Constitution, besides being the first Senator elected to Congress from the State of Delaware. He resigned his seat in the Senate in 1792.

James Ashton Bayard, son of John, was grandfather to Thomas F. Bayard, and with him began the senatorial line of the family name in Congress. He was the acknowledged leader of the old Federal party, and was offered the missions to both France and Russia, but declined. He, however, served as joint commissioner with Clay, Gallatin, Adams, and Russell in negotiating the treaty of Ghent.

Richard H. Bayard was chosen United States Senator in 1836. James Ashton Bayard represented Delaware in the Senate from 1851 to 1864, and retired in 1869, when he was succeeded by his son, the subject of our sketch.

Thomas F. Bayard was born at Wilmington, Del., October 29, 1828; was educated at the Flushing school, established by Rev. Mr. F. L. Hawks. His early training was in the direction of a mercantile life; but he preferred and studied the profession of the law, and was admitted to the bar in 1851. With the exception of two years in Philadelphia, Mr. Bayard practised his profession in his native city. In 1853, he was appointed United States district attorney for the State of Delaware, but resigned in 1854. He was elected United States Senator from Delaware for the term commencing in 1869 and ending in 1875, serving on the important committees on Finance, Judiciary, Private Land Claims, and that on the Revision of Laws, and was a member of the Electoral Commission of 1877. On the same day of his election his father, James A. Bayard, was also re-elected to the Senate from the same State, to fill an unexpired term, the first and only instance recorded of father and son both occupying seats in that august body. Mr. Bayard was re-elected in 1875, and again in 1881, and was appointed Secretary of State by Mr. Cleveland in 1885. He was Senator from Delaware for sixteen years, being the oldest in continuous service of the Democratic Senators. He was chosen President of the Senate, *pro tempore*, Oct. 10, 1881.

Mr. Bayard is a man whose public and private record is of the purest and most honorable character. As a public speaker, he is always listened to with the greatest respect and interest. He had achieved a reputation as a sound and reliable financial authority, prior to assuming the chair of the State Department The result of his administration of the State Department will be best understood from a perusal of the following facts, which are also indicative of that complete success in connection with our foreign relations which is so clearly shown in all other Departments of the Government under the present Administration.

The State Department is recognized as the first among the different departments, and the Secretary of State, in his position as Premier of the Administration, enjoys prerogatives not common to other members of the Cabinet, and is charged with special duties of an official, ceremonial and social nature. He greets, in the name of the President, a member of a Royal family or Ruler of a foreign State visiting the capital. Is present during his call of etiquette and attends the President in returning the visit. He arranges the audiences accorded Diplomatic Ministers in presenting their credentials or taking leave.

The special work of the State Department, under the able administration of the present Secretary and during the past three years and a half, has been to secure through proper diplomatic measures a continuance of friendly relations with all foreign Governments; to carefully guard the citizenship of all native born or naturalized citizens, in whatever part of the world they may be; to maintain our rights whenever attacked, as far as they are known to be just and based upon international law. Under the present Administration, our treaty with the Empire of China has been completed to the satisfaction of all concerned; and while doing justice to all honorable claims on the part of the great Government of the West, at the same time the complaints of our fellow-citizens have been fairly considered, and the result obtained through the work of the State Department is considered most creditable. The Fisheries Treaty, as it is commonly called, is the result of the meeting of Commissioners from Great Britain and the United States, who, after fairly and carefully considering all questions before them, mutually agreed upon a treaty which is now before the United States Senate for confirmation. As much curiosity has been expressed regarding this document, it has been thought best to publish the views of the President upon the subject, as indicated in his Message to the Senate, from which the injunction of secrecy has recently been removed and which we now print in full.

MESSAGE FROM THE PRESIDENT OF THE UNITED STATES, TRANSMITTING A TREATY BETWEEN THE UNITED STATES AND GREAT BRITAIN CONCERNING THE INTERPRETATION OF THE CONVENTION OF OCTOBER 20, 1818, SIGNED AT WASHINGTON, FEBRUARY 15, 1888.

To the Senate of the United States:

In my annual message transmitted to the Congress in December, 1886, it was stated that negotiations were then pending for the settlement of the questions growing out of the rights claimed by American fishermen in British North American waters.

As a result of such negotiations, a treaty has been agreed upon between her Britannic Majesty and the United States, concluded and signed in this capital, under my direction and authority, on the 15th of February instant, and which I now have the honor to submit to the Senate, with the recommendation that it shall receive the consent of that body, as provided in the Constitution, in order that the ratifications thereof may be duly exchanged and the treaty be carried into effect.

Shortly after Congress had adjourned in March last, and in continuation of my efforts to arrive at such an agreement between the Governments of Great Britain and the United States as would secure to the citizens of the respective countries the unmolested enjoyment of their just rights under existing treaties and international comity in the territorial waters of Canada and of Newfoundland, I availed myself of opportune occurrences indicative of a desire to make without delay an amicable and final settlement of a long-standing controversy — productive of much irritation and misunderstanding between the two nations — to send through our minister in London proposals that a conference should take place on the subject at this capital.

The experience of the past two years had demonstrated the dilatory and unsatisfactory consequences of our indirect transaction of business through the foreign office in London, in which the views and wishes of the Government of the Dominion of Canada were practically predominant, but were only to find expression at second hand.

To obviate this inconvenience and obstruction to prompt and well-defined settlement, it was considered advisable that the negotiations should be conducted in this city, and that the interests of Canada and Newfoundland should be directly represented therein.

The terms of reference having been duly agreed upon between the two Governments, and the conference arranged to be held here, by virtue of the power in me vested by the Constitution, I duly authorized Thomas F. Bayard, the Secretary of State of the United States, William L. Putnam, a citizen of the State of Maine, and James B. Angell, a citizen of the State of Michigan, for and in the name of the United States, to meet and confer with the plenipotentiaries representing the Government of her Britannic Majesty, for the purpose of considering and adjusting in a friendly spirit all or any questions relating to rights of fishery in the seas adjacent to British North America and Newfoundland which were in dispute between the Governments of the United States and that of her Britannic Majesty, and jointly and severally to conclude and sign any treaty or treaties touching the premises; and I herewith transmit for your information full copies of the power so given by me.

In execution of the powers so conveyed, the said Thomas F. Bayard, William L. Putnam, and James B. Angell, in the month of November last, met in this city the plenipotentiaries of her

Britannic Majesty, and proceeded in the negotiation of a treaty as above authorized. After many conferences and protracted efforts an agreement has at length been arrived at, which is embodied in the treaty which I now lay before you.

The treaty meets my approval, because I believe that it supplies a satisfactory, practical, and final adjustment, upon a basis honorable and just to both parties, of the difficult and vexed question to which it relates.

A review of the history of this question will show that all former attempts to arrive at a common interpretation, satisfactory to both parties, of the first article of the treaty of October 20, 1818, have been unsuccessful; and with the lapse of time the difficulty and obscurity have only increased.

The negotiations in 1854, and again in 1871, ended in both cases in temporary reciprocal arrangements of the tariffs of Canada and Newfoundland and of the United States, and the payment of a money award by the United States, under which the real questions in difference remained unsettled, in abeyance, and ready to present themselves anew just so soon as the conventional arrangements were abrogated.

The situation, therefore, remained unimproved by the results of the treaty of 1871, and a grave condition of affairs, presenting almost identically the same features and causes of complaint by the United States against Canadian action and British default in its correction, confronted us in May, 1886, and has continued until the present time.

The greater part of the correspondence which has taken place between the two governments has heretofore been communicated to Congress, and at as early a day as possible I shall transmit the remaining portion to this date, accompanying it with the joint protocols of the conferences which resulted in the conclusion of the treaty now submitted to you.

You will thus be fully possessed of the record and history of the case since the termination, on June 30, 1885, of the fishery-articles of the Treaty of Washington of 1871, whereby we were relegated to the provisions of the treaty of October 20, 1818.

As the documents and papers referred to will supply full information of the positions taken under my administration by the representatives of the United States, as well as those occupied by the representatives of the Government of Great Britain, it is not considered necessary or expedient to repeat them in this message. But I believe the treaty will be found to contain a just, honorable, and, therefore, satisfactory solution of the difficulties which have clouded our relations with our neighbors on our northern border.

Especially satisfactory do I believe the proposed arrangement will be found by those of our citizens who are engaged in the open sea fisheries, adjacent to the Canadian coast, and resorting to those ports and harbors under treaty provisions and rules of international law.

The proposed delimitation of the lines of the exclusive fisheries from the common fisheries will give certainty and security as to the area of their legitimate field; the headland theory of imaginary lines is abandoned by Great Britain, and the specification in the treaty of certain named bays especially provided for gives satisfaction to the inhabitants of the shores, without subtracting materially from the value or convenience of the fishery rights of Americans.

The uninterrupted navigation of the Strait of Canso is expressly and for the first time affirmed, and the four purposes for which our fishermen under the treaty of 1818 were allowed to enter the bays and harbors of Canada and Newfoundland within the belt of 3 marine miles are placed under a fair and liberal construction, and their enjoyment secured without such conditions and restrictions as in the past have embarrassed and obstructed them so seriously.

The enforcement of penalties for unlawfully fishing or preparing to fish within the inshore and exclusive waters of Canada and Newfoundland is to be accomplished under safe-guards against oppressive or arbitrary action, thus protecting the defendant fishermen from punishment in advance of trial, delays, and inconvenience and unnecessary expense.

The history of events in the last two years shows that no feature of Canadian administration was more harassing and injurious than the compulsion upon our fishing vessels to make formal entry and clearance on every occasion of temporarily seeking shelter in Canadian ports and harbors.

Such inconvenience is provided against in the proposed treaty, and this most frequent and just cause of complaint is removed.

The articles permitting our fishermen to obtain provisions and the ordinary supplies of trading vessels on their homeward voyages, and under which they are accorded the further and even more important privilege on all occasions of purchasing such casual or needful provisions and supplies as are ordinarily granted to trading vessels, are of great importance and value.

The licenses which are to be granted without charge and on application, in order to enable our fishermen to enjoy these privileges, are reasonable and proper checks in the hands of the local authorities to identify the recipients and prevent abuse, and can form no impediment to those who intend to use them fairly.

The hospitality secured for our vessels in all cases of actual distress, with liberty to unload and sell and transship their cargoes, is full and liberal.

These provisions will secure the substantial enjoyment of the treaty rights for our fishermen under the treaty of 1818, for which contention has been steadily made in the correspondence of the Department of State, and our minister at London, and by the American negotiators of the present treaty.

The right of our fishermen under the treaty of 1818 did not extend to the procurement of distinctive fishery supplies in Canadian ports and harbors; and one item supposed to be essential, to wit, bait, was plainly denied them by the explicit and definite words of the treaty of 1818, emphasized by the course of the negotiation and express decisions which preceded the conclusion of that treaty.

The treaty now submitted contains no provision affecting tariff duties, and, independently of the position assumed upon the part of the United States that no alteration in our tariff or other domestic legislation could be made as the price or consideration of obtaining the rights of our citizens secured by treaty, it was considered more expedient to allow any change in the revenue laws of the United States to be made by the ordinary exercise of legislative will, and in promotion of the public interests. Therefore, the addition to the free list of fish, fish-oil, whale and seal oil, etc., recited in the last article of the treaty, is wholly left to the action of Congress; and in connection therewith the Canadian and Newfoundland right to regulate sales of bait and other fishing supplies within their own jurisdiction is recognized, and the right of our fishermen to freely purchase these things is made contingent, by this treaty, upon the action of Congress in the modification of our tariff laws.

Our social and commercial intercourse with those populations who have been placed upon our borders and made forever our neighbors is made apparent by a list of United States common carriers, marine and inland, connecting their lines with Canada, which was returned by the Secretary of the Treasury to the

Senate on the 7th day of February, 1888, in answer to a resolution of that body; and this is instructive as to the great volume of mutually profitable interchanges which has come into existence during the last half century.

This intercourse is still but partially developed, and if the amicable enterprise and wholesome rivalry between the two populations be not obstructed, the promise of the future is full of the fruits of an unbounded prosperity on both sides of the border.

The treaty now submitted to you has been framed in a spirit of liberal equity and reciprocal benefits, in the conviction that mutual advantage and convenience are the only permanent foundation of peace and friendship between States, and that with the adoption of the agreement now placed before the Senate, a beneficial and satisfactory intercourse between the two countries will be established so as to secure perpetual peace and harmony.

In connection with the treaty herewith submitted I deem it also my duty to transmit to the Senate a written offer or arrangement, in the nature of a *modus vivendi*, tendered after the conclusion of the treaty on the part of the British plenipotentiaries, to secure kindly and peaceful relations during the period that may be required for the consideration of the treaty by the respective Governments and for the enactmemt of the necessary legislation to carry its provisions into effect if approved.

This paper, freely and on their own motion, signed by the British conferees, not only extends advantages to our fishermen, pending the ratification of the treaty, but appears to have been dictated by a friendly and amicable spirit.

I am given to understand that the other governments concerned in this treaty will, within a few days, in accordance with their methods of conducting public business, submit said treaty to their respective legislatures, when it will be at once published to the world. In view of such action it appears to be advisable that, by publication here, early and full knowledge of all that has been done in the premises should be afforded to our people.

It would also seem to be useful to inform the popular mind concerning the history of the long continued disputes growing out of the subject embraced in the treaty and to satisfy the public interests touching the same, as well as to acquaint our people with the present status of the questions involved, and to give them the exact terms of the proposed adjustment, in place of the exaggerated and imaginative statements which will otherwise reach them.

I therefore beg leave respectfully to suggest that said treaty and all such correspondence, messages, and documents relating to the same as may be deemed important to accomplish these purposes be at once made public by the order of your honorable body.

GROVER CLEVELAND.

EXECUTIVE MANSION,
February 20, 1888.

We are confident that upon the careful reading of the preceding document every sensible man will acknowledge, that the rights of our fishermen are carefully preserved, and that the attacks of partisan politicians upon an honorable decision, arrived at by the combined judgment of able and experienced men, are totally unwarranted, and it is to be hoped that the usually clear-sightedness of United States Senators will recognize the facts in the case and that they govern themselves accordingly. It is a matter for grave consideration and thankfulness on the part of every American citizen, that through the able management of the State Department, under its present head, that this nation has been preserved from war and the rumors of war, which, had it been under the control of a less conservative man, might have led this country into a conflict which we are not prepared to meet. This Administration is one of peace, and the experience of the past four years is sufficient to make us all look forward with confidence to a continuance of such management as will leave our people time to do justice to their agricultural, manufacturing, mercantile, and commercial pursuits.

Our present relations with all the world are satisfactory and the United States to-day holds a position which should make every American citizen thank God for the advantages which he enjoys.

As arbitrator of difficulties between other nations the aid of the President has been secured, and through the action of the State Department these decisions have been rendered to the satisfaction of the contending parties. The great value and importance of our consular system, in its connection with the growth of our manufactures and the increase of trade and commerce by the introduction of new channels, has been fully recognized by the present Secretary of the State Department, not only by presenting to Congress the absolute need of a more satisfactory system of payment for the work done, but also in supplying the public with weekly instalments of information from our consuls in all parts of the world. These reports being regularly supplied to the press become public property and are at once utilized when available to the general advantage of the public.

The business of the State Department is kept thoroughly in hand, each bureau completing its work daily, and at the present time there is no accumulated work. This is due to the management adopted by the Secretary and the persevering labors of those employed. In the organization and systematized work of the State Department will be found additional evidence that the present Administration is established on a business basis.

C. S. Fairchild

CHAPTER VI.

THE TREASURY DEPARTMENT.

The Secretary of the Treasury is charged by law with the management of the national finances. He prepares plans for the improvement of the revenue and for the support of the public credit; superintends the collection of the revenue, and prescribes the forms of keeping and rendering public accounts and of making returns; grants warrants for all moneys drawn from the Treasury in pursuance of appropriations made by law, and for the payment of moneys into the Treasury; and annually submits to Congress estimates of the probable revenues and disbursements of the Government. He also controls the construction of public buildings; the coinage and printing of money; the collection of statistics; the administration of the coast and geodetic survey; life-saving, light-house, revenue-cutter, steamboat inspection, and marine-hospital branches of the public service; and furnishes generally such information as may be required by either branch of Congress on all matters pertaining to the foregoing.

The routine work of the Secretary's office is transacted in the offices of the Supervising Architect, Director of the Mint, Superintendent of Engraving and Printing, Supervising Surgeon-General of Marine Hospitals, General Superintendent of Life-Saving Service, Supervising Inspector-General of Steamboats, Bureau of Statistics, Light-House Board, and in the following divisions: Warrants, Estimates, and Appropriations; Appointments; Customs; Public Moneys; Loans and Currency; Mercantile Marine and Internal Revenue; Revenue-Marine; Stationery, Printing, and Blanks; Captured Property, Claims, and Lands; Mails and Files, and Special Agents.

THE SECRETARY OF THE TREASURY.

CHARLES S. FAIRCHILD.

Sidney T. Fairchild, the father of the present Secretary of the Treasury, is known as one of the most distinguished lawyers of Central New York. He was for many years leading counsel for the New York Central Railroad Company. Charles S. Fairchild was born at Cazenovia, Madison County, New York, April 30, 1842. He received his elementary education at the Methodist seminary in that town, from which he graduated in 1850. He immediately entered Harvard College, where he graluated in 1863, and afterwards graduated from the Law School in 1865. Having completed his collegiate and legal education, he became junior member of the law firm of Hand, Hale, Schwartz & Fairchild, in Albany, one of the leading firms in the State of New York. In 1868 he began his political career by organizing the Democratic party of his native county, as chairman of its committee, in support of Horatio Seymour for President, Mr. Fairchild running for the State Senate himself. In 1874, he was appointed Deputy Attorney General by the Hon. Daniel Pratt, and in that important office was concerned in many famous cases, especially in relation to the removal of the police commissioners of the city of New York, when he was opposed by the leading counsel of the State and city, but succeeded in his efforts to secure for New York city the purity of elections.

During the Canal Ring investigations in New York, Mr. Fairchild was closely associated with Samuel J. Tilden, who had great confidence in his judgment and abilities and always favored his political advancement. He is sound on financial questions and supports the Administration in its position in connection with silver, and tariff reform.

As a recognition of his ability he was nominated and elected Attorney General in 1876. Having served out his term he spent two years in Europe. He was President of the Charities Aid Association of the State and Vice-President of the Charity Organization Society of the City of New York.

City, where he remained until invited to the second place in the administration of the Treasury Department by Secretary Manning. Mr. Fairchild became Secretary of the Treasury by appointment of the President in 1887.

Secretary Fairchild is a man of quick perceptions and an analytical mind. He is one of the seven youngest persons who have filled the post of Secretary of the Treasury. The youngest was Alexander Hamilton, Washington's first secretary, who was thirty-two; Wolcott, the second, was thirty-five; Dexter and Gallatin, third and fourth, were forty; Brewster was forty-one; Crawford and Fairchild were each forty-four.

In his management of the Treasury Department, Mr. Fairchild has secured the confidence of both the Government and the people; and the important results of his careful and conscientious labor as herewith given will prove that he is fully entitled to the great confidence thus secured.

THE TREASURY DEPARTMENT. 121

The most important work of this department obviously consists of the collection of the revenues, and the management of the national finances.

In the matter of the collection of the revenue, which is mainly derived from receipts for customs dues and from internal taxes, it will be seen, from an examination of the records and reports of the department, that there has been a steady and decided increase of revenue, and a steady and decided *decrease* of the cost of collection, under the present Administration. The fiscal year ends on the thirtieth day of June, and the present year, therefore, completes three full fiscal years of this administration of the department; and beginning with the fiscal year 1884, which was the first year after the tariff law of 1883 went into effect, it will be found that the receipts from customs for that year were, in round numbers, one hundred and ninety-five millions of dollars; for 1885, one hundred and eighty-one millions of dollars; for 1886, one hundred and ninety-three millions of dollars,—being the first year of this administration,—an increase of twelve millions of dollars; and in 1887 they were two hundred and seventeen millions of dollars, a further increase of twenty-five millions; and for 1888, two hundred and twenty millions of dollars, a further increase of three millions, making a total increase during the three years of over forty millions of dollars; while the cost of collection for 1884 was .0344 per cent; 1885, .0377 per cent; 1886, .0330 per cent; 1887, .0316 per cent; 1888, .0298 per cent.

The same results are shown in the receipts from internal revenue, and the expenditures in that branch of the service: the collections for the fiscal year 1885, being, in round numbers, one hundred and twelve millions; 1886, one hundred and seventeen millions; 1887, one hundred and nineteen millions; 1888, one hundred and twenty-five millions, a total increase of thirteen millions of dollars; while the cost of collection has decreased from .03963 per cent for 1885 to .0302 per cent in 1888. This has been accomplished notwithstanding that the work of collecting the tax upon oleomargarine, and the enforcement of the law against the illicit production and traffic in that article, have, during this period, been devolved upon the Internal Revenue Bureau.

In both the customs and internal revenue service, great vigilance has been displayed in the detection and suppression of frauds upon the revenue. In the customs department especial attention has been given to the subject of undervaluations, which had grown to be so great an abuse that loud complaints were constantly made by the domestic manufacturer and the honest importer, that their business was seriously imperilled in consequence of it. The result has been that this abuse has been practically eradicated, and save in rare instances are complaints now made either to the department or in the public press upon that account. Greater promptness in the transaction of customs business has also been secured. Two-thirds of the revenue from customs are collected at the port of New York; and two years ago the work of the Liquidating Division at that port was over two years behind, and the Division of Protests and Appeals was equally in arrears; but at the present time the work of both divisions has been so far advanced, that, by the end of this calender year, all arrears of business will have been disposed of, and the work will be up to current date.

In the matter of the management of the national finances a brief review of some of the difficulties which had to be encountered, and of the dangers which threatened the country, and of the manner in which they have been avoided and averted, will satisfy every candid and impartial mind that this branch of the public service was never more ably or more faithfully administered.

On the 30th of June, 1887, the surplus in the Treasury, according to the Treasurer's statement of assets and liabilities, was $45,698,594.15. The expenditures, actual and estimated, including the sinking-fund, for the fiscal year 1888 were $316,817,785.48; and the revenues of the Government for the same period, under existing tariff and revenue laws, were estimated to be approximately $383,000,000. Thus an addition to the surplus during the fiscal year of $66,182,214.52 was expected, making the total surplus on the 30th of June, 1888, $111,880,808.67. This was the situation as it appeared one year ago. It will be seen from what follows that the estimate was far below the reality.

Early in August, 1887, it became apparent that the rapid accumulation of money in the Treasury, which had already created a feeling of great anxiety and uneasiness in business centres, would soon cause severe stringency in the money markets. The time was approaching when the annual shipments of money to the West for the purpose of moving the crops would deplete the reserves in the great cities. This depletion, which in good crop years is always great enough to increase the loaning rate to seven per cent and upward, threatened to be so great as to cripple the movement of money so necessary to the welfare of the country, particularly of the great grain-raising sections of the West; and the constantly increasing surplus in the Treasury was daily adding to the gravity of the situation. At this juncture the Secretary of the Treasury wisely determined, that, instead of distributing the purchases for the sinking-fund over the whole fiscal year as he would do in ordinary circumstances, he would invest the entire amount (nearly twenty-eight millions) at once, or as rapidly as possible; hoping thereby to so far relieve the impending distress as to tide over the period of moving the crops, and so prevent business disturbances during that critical time. To this end he published the circular of August, 1887, and later the circular of September, 1887, for the purchase of bonds for the sinking-fund. The first circular proposed to receive offers weekly, at prices to be named by the owners; and when all which were offered at fair prices had been obtained by that method, the second circular was published, fixing a price at which they would be received. Under these two circulars the Secretary purchased $24,844,650 bonds at a cost of $27,842,237.10. No comment is needed to emphasize the importance and vast benefit of this operation. The Secretary placed in the hands of the people nearly twenty-eight millions of money with which to carry on the most important business transactions of the year. The wisdom and success of this measure is best shown by the fact, that, throughout the period when the greatest trouble has heretofore occurred, not the slightest disturbance of business was recorded, and the average rate paid for money on call in New York, the great banking centre of the country, was never lower.

Upon completing the purchase of bonds for the sinking-fund, the question of disposing of the further additions to the surplus was carefully considered. The authority to purchase bonds in addition to the sinking-fund requirements was not considered to be so clear and unequivocal as to justify the Secretary in making purchases.

The authority, such as it was, was contained in a paragraph in the Legislative Appropriation Bill, approved March 3, 1881; and, after a careful survey of all the circumstances, it was decided that doubt existed, and that all other lawful means should first be exhausted before resorting to other purchases. The only resource left appeared to be in the Secretary's authority to use national banks as depositories of public money. Prior to this time, the deposits in national banks had been somewhat restricted by the unprofitable nature of the terms offered to the banks. They were limited to a deposit of 90 per cent of the par value of the bonds deposited by them as security, so that from 18 to 36 per cent of the value of the bonds was practically locked up. In view of the high premium which these bonds commanded as an investment, it was decided to allow a deposit of the par value of $4\frac{1}{2}$ per cent bonds held as security, and a deposit of 110 per cent against 4 per cent bonds held. The result is best shown by the following statement : —

On the 1st of July, 1885, there were 141 national banks whose designations as depositories were in force, and the deposits of public moneys in their hands amounted to $12,928,264.47. On the 1st of July, 1888, there were 294 banks holding public deposits of $59,979,039.63. This is an increase of 153 banks, and an increase of deposits in their hands of $47,050,775.16. In other words, there are more than twice as many banks now acting as depositories as there were three years ago, and they hold nearly five times as much public money as they did three years ago. This great sum of $47,000,000 is now in the hands of the people as the result of the wise and liberal policy of the Secretary, instead of remaining locked up in the Treasury as it would have remained under the policy formerly in operation; and the security held for the safe return to the Treasury of the money deposited is at all times ample, for the 4½ per cent bonds held by the Treasury have at all times been worth at least .7 per cent more than the deposit, and the 4 per cent at least 15 per cent more. Either class of bonds can be sold at a day's notice, so that no possible contingency could result in loss to the Government. The efforts of the Secretary to keep down the surplus in the Treasury were effectual during the fall and early winter, but the time soon came when something more must be done; for the surplus continued to grow, and the measures which had been so effective earlier in the fiscal year were now inoperative, from causes which were clearly foreseen, and to which the present Secretary and his able predecessor, Mr. Manning, had repeatedly called the attention of Congress without avail. The absorption of public moneys by the depository banks had reached its limit, and the sinking-fund requirements had been supplied; so that nothing remained to be done but to await the action of Congress. There had been discussion of the subject in both houses, but no material progress towards a settlement of the question had been made. In April, however, the House passed a resolution declaratory of its judgment that the clause in the appropriation bill of March 3, 1881, was still in force; and a similar resolution was passed a few days later in the Senate. The sanction of Congress having thus been practically given to the policy of purchasing unmatured obligations at a premium, the Secretary promptly on the day after the passage of the Senate resolution published a circular, dated April 17, 1888, inviting daily offerings of bonds to the Government. This circular, like those which preceded it in August and September, 1887, invited the people to deal directly with the Government in selling their bonds, being a marked departure from the policy of former Administrations in this respect. All previous purchases had been made through the sub-treasury in New York, and a deposit as a guaranty of good faith was required. This restriction placed the business of selling bonds to the Government exclusively in the hands of the professional dealers in securities, and consequently placed individual holders at their mercy. Under the present system, the humblest citizen of the United States, owner of a bond for fifty dollars, can deal directly with the Government; and his proposal for the sale of his bond receives from the Secretary the same consideration, and if his bond is accepted the same prompt payment, as that accorded the dealer who sells his millions at a time.

Under this circular of April 17, 1888, the Secretary had purchased up to June 30, 1888, $18,383,800

4 per cent bonds at a cost of $23,347,744.20, and $8,393,050 4½ per cent at a cost of $9,039,056.20, making a total disbursement on acccount of purchase of $32,386,800.40.

The bonds so purchased, it should be remembered, were not redeemable; the 4½ per cents being payable after September, 1891, and the 4 per cents not until after July 1, 1907.

The amount, therefore, which the Government would pay in interest and principal on the bonds if outstanding till maturity would be for the 4½ per cents $9,705,158.31, and for the 4 per cents $32,539,326, making a total of $42,244,484.31. The difference between this amount and the amount actually paid results in a direct saving to the Government of $9,857,683.91, which, added to savings in 1887 of $4,832,668.62, makes a total saving of $14,790,352.03; so that at the same time that the Secretary of the Treasury was relieving the people by disbursing the money they so badly needed, he was saving to them nearly $15,000,000, and making possible a still further reduction of taxation to that amount.

But, notwithstanding the utmost endeavors of the Secretary to diminish the surplus, statements published at the close of the fiscal year 1888 show that it is larger than at the commencement of the purchases in August, 1887. According to the statements of assets and liabilities for Aug. 1, 1887, the surplus was then $45,698,594.15; and on July 1, 1888, it was $103,220,464.71, which is an increase of $57,521,870.56, notwithstanding the purchase during the interval of United States bonds costing over $32,000,000, in addition to those purchased in

August for the sinking-fund, and which were included in the estimated expenditures for the fiscal year.

At the beginning of this statement it was shown that the estimates made on June 20, 1887, for the ensuing fiscal year indicated a probable surplus of $111,880,808.67 during the year. The actual surplus was $135,607,265.11, consisting of $103,220,464.71 still in the Treasury, and $32,386,800.40 paid for bonds purchased. This is an increase over the estimate of $23,726,456.44.

There has prevailed the belief that the accumulation of the surplus revenues in the Treasury, and the retirement of national bank notes by banks reducing circulation, must result in contraction of the circulation of the country. So far the wise, prudent, and skilful management of the Government finances by the Secretary of the Treasury has averted all trouble from this source. Indeed, the amount of money in circulation among the people to-day is greater than it was two years ago. The total circulation Jan. 1, 1886, was $1,285,173,012; while the amount June 30, 1888, was $1,372,627,868, an *increase* of $87,454,856.

The following table shows how this increase is effected.

CHANGES.

	Increase.	*Decrease.*
Gold Coin	$38,625,381	
Silver Dollars	3,287,732	
Subsidiary Coin	3,207,372	
Gold Certificates	14,527,769	
Silver Certificates	107,207,911	
United States Notes		$10,042,004
National Bank Notes		69,359,305
	$166,856,165	$79,401,309

At the time the present Administration assumed the charge of the Treasury Department, very grave apprehensions were entertained by eminent financiers, that gold and silver could not be maintained as currency upon equal footing; and it was believed in many quarters that they must soon part company, and that gold would soon become the sole standard of value in the commerce of the country. It was claimed that such a result must follow from the Act requiring the compulsory purchase and coinage of silver by the Government at the rate of at least two million dollars per month; and it may be fairly urged that such would have been the inevitable consequence had it not been for the determination of the Treasury Department to use all lawful expedients to maintain the equality of the two metals as to their purchasing power, and the wise policy inaugurated and pursued by it in this respect. How completely successful it has been, the above exhibit will show. There has been an increase in eighteen months of over $110,000,000 in the silver circulation of the country; thereby not only placing in the hands of the people the $36,000,000 of silver coined during that period, but also over $74,000,000 of the accumulated silver in the Treasury.

Every American citizen is justly proud of the rapidity with which the great public debt of the country is reduced from year to year, and the record of this Administration far surpasses all its predecessors in this respect. The average annual reduction of the public debt during the three years preceding June 30, 1885, being $99,500,000; and during the three years succeeding the same date, $106,500,000.

Another important branch of the work of the Treasury Department is the auditing and adjustment of public accounts. The annual expenditures of the Government for all purposes exceed three hundred millions of dollars, not a dollar of which expenditure can be legally allowed until an account therefor has been rendered to the proper accounting officers of the Treasury Department, and the same has been approved and certified by them to be correct. This work is mainly done by the six auditors, two comptrollers, commissioner of customs, and the various divisions of the Secretary's office. When the present Administration undertook this work, it was in many bureaus and divisions very largely in arrears. It will be impossible in the brief limits of this book to give any thing like a detailed or tabulated statement of the results which have been accomplished here during the past three years. A few prominent facts only can be mentioned.

In the office of the first auditor, where the accounts accruing in the Treasury Department are first examined, during the three years subsequent to 1885 there has been an average annual increase of three thousand in the number of accounts examined and certified as compared with the three years immediately preceding, and an average decrease of the cost of the office, on the basis of the amount of work done, of nearly eleven per cent annually.

In the office of the first comptroller, which reviews in part the accounts examined and certified by the first auditor, and also the accounts of the fifth auditor, there has been an average annual increase, during the same period, in the number of accounts of 7,700, and an increase in the amount involved, as shown by the footings of the accounts examined, of nearly one billion dollars annually; and the average decrease of cost of work has been about twenty-one per cent annually.

In the office of the fourth auditor, where all the disbursements in the naval service are first examined, there has been an average annual increase of forty per cent in the number of claims and accounts adjusted, and of over nine millions in the amount involved; while the average annual expenses of the office have been over two thousand dollars less, and an average decrease in the cost of work, according to the amount done, of thirty-five per cent annually.

In the office of the commissioner of customs there has been an increase of eleven per cent in the average number of accounts annually adjusted *per capita;* and in the Division of Customs, in the Secretary's office, in which all the appeals in customs cases from the decision of collectors are examined and reported upon, there were examined and decided during the fiscal year ending June 30, 1886, 25,537 appeals, while the total number for the three years immediately preceding only aggregated 26,526; it thus appearing that the work for the entire three years was only slightly in excess of that of the single year 1886.

In the office of the sixth auditor, where all the accounts of the Post-office Department, and the expenditures of the postal service, amounting to over fifty millions of dollars annually, are finally adjusted, a corresponding improvement in the methods of transacting the public business has been effected. Much money has been saved to the public Treasury by the more rigid scrutiny to which the accounts passing through this office have been subjected. As an illustration, it may be stated that the number of cases in which orders have been made by the Postmaster-General, upon the report of the auditor, withholding commissions because of false reports of postmasters to increase their compensation, is 571, charging back an aggregate of $228,815; and it is evident, from an examination of the books, that the probable loss to the Government during the period from 1878 to 1885 was more than one million of dollars from this single channel of fraud.

In the second auditor's office are first examined the accounts of the disbursing officers of the army, and all claims for the back pay and bounty of soldiers in the war of the Rebellion, and all disbursements in the Indian service for supplies and the pay of agents and other officers. During the past three years there has been an increase in the number of claims and accounts adjusted of over thirty per cent, and an increase of over forty per cent in the amount involved, over a corresponding period prior to June 30, 1885; and the amount allowed and paid out for the back pay and bounty due soldiers during the last three years has been over $2,700,000, as against only $1,350,000 allowed in the three previous years, showing that the interests of the soldiers of the Union army have received special attention and consideration.

The third auditor has the examination, in the first instance, of all claims and accounts arising in the Quartermaster's and Commissary Departments of the army, including horse claims and miscellaneous claims and accounts, and all disbursements on account of pensions. The exhibit of work done in this office during the past three years, it is believed, is without parallel in the history of the department. In the Claims Division over 41,000 claims have been disposed of during that period, while during the three years previously only 11,000 were adjusted; making an increase of over 350 per cent, and the amount involved was over 100 per cent greater. In the Horse-Claims Division over 9,000 claims were disposed of during the past three years, and but 2,200 in the three years previously, an increase of over 400 per cent. In State war claims there has been an increase of nearly 700 per cent in the amount of claims disposed of during the same periods respectively, and in the Pension Division there has been an average increase in the work of the division of 254 per cent during the past three years over the work of the three previous years, and an average decrease in the force amounting to 31 per cent. During the past three years the number of clerks employed has been *reduced* 21 per cent, and great improvement is noted in the attendance of clerks. The absences in the fiscal years 1884–85 aggregated over 6,000 days, while in 1887–88 there were only 3,750 days; and during the same years the absence on account of sickness fell off from 1780 to 357 days.

The work of the second comptroller's office exhibits exceptionally good results. This office has the final revision and adjustment of all claims and accounts which are first examined in the offices of the second, third, and fourth auditors, and the supervision of the expenditures of all the appropriations for the army, the navy, the Indian service, and the pension roll, aggregating over $150,000,000 annually. The average number of claims and accounts annually adjusted during the past three years is over 51,000, while the number was but 22,000 annually during the three years prior to 1885, an increase of 133 per cent; and the number of vouchers examined and compared during the former period was 7,300,000, and but 3,600,000 during the years 1882, 1883, and 1884; and the official letters written were 22,000 as against 5,200 during the same periods respectively, while at the same time the force of clerks actually employed in the office has been *reduced* one-third.

The office of the supervising architect of the Treasury Department has charge of all matters relating to the erection of public buildings throughout the country under appropriations by Acts of Congress. It has been under the supervision of the present supervising architect since July, 1887; and during that period many reforms have been introduced into the administration of the office, and a large saving of expenses effected. The preparation of specifications has been greatly simplified; and where, under the former system, 380 drawings and 51 specifications were prepared for four buildings, under the present method only 86 drawings and 4 specifications are required for the same buildings. Greater competition in submitting proposals has also been secured by giving greater publicity to the advertisements for proposals, especially by securing their publication, free of cost to the Government, in eighteen building papers published in all parts of the country, and obtaining the co-operation of forty-three building exchanges located in the principal cities. Where but three or four proposals were formerly received, the number now has run up in one case as high as forty-four. During the past year work has been commenced on seventeen buildings, and ten buildings have been completed, and twelve buildings are now so far advanced that they will be completed before Sept. 1; while during the three preceding years the average number of buildings commenced annually was ten, and the average number completed annually, four. These results have all been accomplished without any increase in the working force of the office.

In the Bureau of Engraving and Printing there has been a great increase in the amount of work done, and a great saving in the cost of doing it. In the three years ending June 30, 1885, there were produced 91,754,351 sheets of securities at a cost of $3,047,483.75. In the three years ending June 30, 1888, 97,346,662 sheets of securities were turned out at a cost of $2,542,505.07. The increase in the number of securities printed was 5,592,311, and the saving in expense $504,978.68. The average cost of a thousand sheets of securities in 1885 was $34.21; in 1888 it was only $24.94. 38,038,939 sheets of securities in 1888 cost $948,819.29. The greatest production in any prior year was in 1883, when 33,330,746 sheets cost $1,104,986.43. In 1885 the average number of employees was 1,133, and the average number of sheets turned out for each employee less than 25,000. In 1888 the average number of employees was 895, and the average number of sheets produced by each employee 42,500.

These results have been due to economies in the management of the bureau, simpler methods of doing business, the discharge of superfluous employees, the doing away with unnecessary places, and the exaction of greater diligence in the discharge of duty, and of a higher standard of qualification. At the same time the quality of the work, especially of the engraving, has been improved; better provision has been made for the health and comfort of the employees, and new and improved machinery has been introduced. A just and orderly system of promotion has been followed, and the employees have had more constant employment and better wages than ever before, while they have been free from the terror of arbitrary dismissal. Under the present Administration not a single person has been discharged for partisan reasons, or to make room for another. Specific appropriations have been secured, fixing the amount to be spent for plate-printing, for other services, and for materials, in lieu of the loose and indefinite appropriations which were formerly the rule; and the number, grades, and salaries of all the employees have been fixed by law or regulation. By a recent order of the President, all the employees of the bureau have been brought under the civil service rules. These measures have made of the Bureau of Engraving and Printing an orderly, efficient, and reputable business establishment, which may safely challenge comparison with any like establishment in the world.

The same general good results may be safely affirmed of every other bureau and division in the department, and there is scarcely a desk in the whole department upon which there can be found any thing but current work; and this condition of the public business has not been reached by slighting work of any kind, but only after the most careful and painstaking examination of every voucher or question involving the law governing the adjustment and settlement of accounts. Nor has it been brought about by increasing the number of clerks and other employees in the department. On the contrary, the pay-roll of nearly every bureau and division shows a material decrease. The number of persons on the rolls of the department at Washington on the first day of July, 1885, was 3,747; and the number on the first day of July, 1888, 3,433. Useless offices have been abolished, and divisions have been consolidated; and a large saving in expenditure has thus been effected, while the efficiency of the service has at the same time been greatly promoted.

CHAPTER VII.

THE WAR DEPARTMENT.

The Secretary of War performs such duties as the President may enjoin upon him concerning the military service, and has the controlling supervision of the purchase of Army supplies, transportation, etc., and of all expenditures made under the appropriations for the support of the Army, and for such of a civil nature as may by law be placed under his administration.

He is required to provide for the taking of meteorological observations at the military stations in the interior of the continent, and at other points in the States and Territories; arranges the course of studies at the Military Academy; submits to Congress all estimates for public buildings and grounds in charge of the Chief of Engineers, and has supervision of all expenditures of appropriations for repair or improvement of the public buildings and grounds in the District of Columbia in charge of the Chief of Engineers. He is charged with the purchase of such real estate as in his judgment is suitable and necessary for the purpose of carrying into effect the provisions for national cemeteries. He exercises supervision of the disbursements by Army officers; has the control and management of the National Park forming a part of Mackinac Island in the State of Michigan, and has direction of the expenditure of the appropriation for the Mississippi River Commission.

He submits annually to Congress a statement of the appropriations for the preceding fiscal year for the Department of War under each specified head of appropriation, the amount expended and remaining on hand, together with estimates of the probable demands that may remain on each appropriation.

He also submits to Congress at each session, in connection with reports of examinations and surveys of rivers and harbors, full statements of all facts tending to show the extent to which the general commerce of the country will be promoted by the several works of improvement contemplated by such examinations and surveys, together with numerous other reports relating to the various matters of which he has supervision.

THE SECRETARY OF WAR.

WILLIAM CROWNINSHIELD ENDICOTT

Is a descendant of John Endicott, who was Governor of the Colony of Massachusetts in 1628, and his family have been continuously residents of Salem and its immediate vicinity ever since, most of the time in the old homestead of Governor Endicott. He is the son of William Putnam Endicott and Mary, daughter of Hon. Jacob Crowninshield, and was born in Salem, Nov. 19, 1826, and was reared and educated in that place. He was fitted for college at Salem, and graduated from Harvard in 1847. Afterwards evincing a desire to choose the law as a profession, he at once entered the office of Nathaniel J. Lord, Esq., of Salem, who then stood at the head of the Essex bar, and, after a course at the Cambridge Law School, he was admitted to practice at Salem in 1850. For the next two years he was alone, but found that he could form a business alliance with J. W. Perry, Esq., whose name is now well known as a legal author. It was during this partnership that Mr. Perry wrote the work which has since become famous and been pronounced one of the ablest works on the subject of which it treats, namely, "Perry on Trusts." In his preface Mr. Perry speaks of Mr. Endicott the following words:

"And it is my especial duty and pleasure to acknowledge my obligations to my friend and associate in business for nearly twenty years, William Crowninshield Endicott, Esq., whose sound learning and clear judgment have been a never-failing resource in matters of doubt and difficulty, and whose refined and severe taste has been freely employed in smoothing redundances and softening asperities of manner and style."

He was a director in one of the old State banks of Salem, and at the age of twenty-nine years he was elected its president, which position he held until the bank went out of existence.

Very soon the abilities of Mr. Endicott as a lawyer were recognized, and this, combined with his deportment and dignity of character, attracted and held a very large and constantly increasing business. So marked was his prominence, both as a lawyer and as a man, that, a vacancy occurring on the bench of the Supreme Judicial Court of Massachusetts in 1873, Governor William B. Washburn selected him, although of a political party opposed to his own, for appointment to the vacant seat, without solicitation on the part of Mr. Endicott or his friends.

He continued on the bench until 1882, when, his health failing him from the very close application to the business of the Court, he was compelled to go abroad, and, after having been in Europe for about a year, he forwarded his resignation to his colleagues upon the bench, whom he requested to place the letter in the hands of the Governor, Hon. John D. Long; but his colleagues did not at once comply with his request, hoping to change his determination, thus retaining his valuable services to the State. The ill-health of Mr. Endicott continuing, he was forced to decline the kindly offices of his colleagues, and insisted upon the prompt deliverance of his letter of resignation to the Governor, which was accordingly done and accepted. And thus, after a period of nearly ten years upon the bench, during which time he delivered four hundred opinions and decisions as a judge, he closed his judicial career.

On his return to the United States, he opened an

office in Boston for the practice of his profession, and became the general counsel for the New England Mutual Life Insurance Company.

In 1884, he was induced, after long and frequent urging, to consent to the use of his name as the Democratic candidate for Governor of the State. He accepted the nomination against his inclinations, as he did not feel equal to the long and protracted labors of a campaign, and with the understanding that under no circumstances was he to be called upon to participate in the campaign.

In February, 1885, he was tendered a position in the Cabinet, in charge of the portfolio of Secretary of War, which position he has held continuously ever since, with credit to himself and honor to the nation.

A distinguished literary gentleman of Massachusetts has paid the following graceful tribute to Mr. Endicott:

"Among the cultivated men of Salem, William C. Endicott has accomplished, as lawyer, writer, jurist, and statesman, a work of which his native city will always be proud. He was born in Salem in 1826, and was graduated at Harvard in 1847. After having taken his degree at Cambridge, he was admitted to the bar in Essex County, and commenced the practice of his profession in Salem. His judgment as a lawyer was soon recognized, and he became one of the leaders of the bar and one of the best of office advisers. The grace and finish of his style have always been recognized in his public performances, among the most interesting and elaborate of which are his orations on the two hundred and fiftieth anniversary of the landing of John Endicott, celebrated in Salem in 1878; his address, before the Young Men's Union on Patriotism as bearing on the duties of the citizens; address on John Hampden and his relations to the great Puritan movement here and in England; lecture on Chivalry; agricultural address at Sterling on the relation of agriculture to the stability and prominence of the State; and speech on the death of N. J. Lord. Mr. Endicott's services on the supreme bench of Massachusetts are highly esteemed, and his conduct of affairs as Secretary of War, to which he was appointed in 1885, will place him on the list of sound and judicious Cabinet Ministers."

The results of his administration of the military affairs of the Government will best be understood by a reference to the pages which follow.

Among the principal acts of Mr. Endicott as Secretary of War was the organization of the Board on Fortifications or Other Defences on June 1, 1885. Meetings were held at New York and elsewhere, during which the defensive works of the United States in the different parts of the country were thoroughly inspected, as well as the capacity of the large number of iron and steel works of the country; numerous papers from inventors and other persons in reference to the subject of fortifications and defences were received and examined and the whole subject of coast defences was dealt with. An exhaustive report of the Board was submitted to Congress, wherein the utterly defenceless condition of the sea-coast and lake frontier is thoroughly set forth, and asking that immediate action be taken to prevent the disastrous and humiliating results that might follow a declaration of war with the most insignificant of foreign powers possessing guns and ships of modern construction.

In connection with this work was that of the examination of the different methods or inventions for the resisting of attacks from the seaboard, and how to best silence the armored ships and steel guns and mortars of modern construction. Among other means of defence which have been developed and examined under the auspices of the Board, is the dynamite gun and others of large calibre that have been tested at Sandy Hook.

Under Mr. Endicott's administration of the War Department, the civil service law has been strictly observed, and in no instances have removals been made in the War Department for purely political reasons; indeed, the removals have been very few, and in every instance for cause. Below is presented a statement showing the changes which occurred in the classified service of the department between July 16, 1883, the date on which the law went into operation, to July 1, 1888, in the belief that it may be of interest and possibly of some value, as showing the practical operation of the law:

Resigned	237
Died	80
Discharged	158
Dropped at the end of probationary term	9
Total	484
Appointed	356
Decrease (through legislation) in number of positions	86
Vacancies existing	42
Total	484

The following statement shows the number of persons to whom letters of appointment were issued, but who failed, for the reasons stated, to enter the service:

Declined appointments	37
Failed to report	10
Died prior to receipt of appointment	1
Total	48

The total number of positions in the classified service in the War Department on November 14, 1887, including twenty-three places exempt from the operations of the law under Rule XIX of the Civil Service Rules, was 1,264. Taking this number as a basis of calculation, it will be seen from the foregoing statement that the aggregate of those resigned and those who failed to accept appointment constituted 19 per cent. of the entire force.

Mr. Endicott has also been an advocate of an increase in the salaries of the efficient clerks, in order to induce them to remain in the public service. If the higher places had higher salaries and were open to competition, it would add much to the efficiency of the service and would hold out strong inducements to the older clerks to remain.

The departmental examinations for promotion under the new Civil Service Rules, which occurred in the summer of 1887 and which were held during the period between June 18 and October 28, embraced the whole classified service of the War Department. The total number of persons examined was 1,014, of whom 953, or 95 per cent., passed the examination, and of this number 353, or 35 per cent., attained an average marking above 90. Of the total number examined 51, or

5 per cent., failed to pass, having attained an average marking of less than 75 per cent.

At the second departmental examination held April 25, 1888, there were examined —

		Failed
Of Class 3	2	—
Of Class 2	21	2
Of Class 1	18	4
Of Class $1,000	46	3
Of Class D	2	—

It thus appears that, of the 89 persons examined, 80 (or 90 per cent.) passed the examination; while 9 (or 10 per cent.) failed to pass, having attained an average marking of less than 75 per cent.

The Secretary believes there are other great advantages resulting from the Civil Service Law, and among them the entire abolition of political assessments and the abandonment of "election leaves," the latter of which had grown into a great abuse. Prior to the enactment of the Civil Service Law in 1883, it was the custom to grant employees of the department leaves of absence to attend the various elections in their several States, and these were not deducted from their annual leaves of thirty days each year, and, for the 1,200 employees of the department, estimating that 50 per cent. took advantage of the election leaves, amounted to 6,000 days, and equalled the time of one clerk for twenty years. Since the passage of the Civil Service Law this custom has ceased to exist. Employes who desire to exercise the elective franchise may still do so, but the time consumed must be deducted from their annual leave of thirty days, thus saving to the government their services.

Through the active and persevering labor of

those connected with the Quartermaster-General's Office, the reforms carried out under the suggestion and approval of the Secretary of War have been very successful, as may be seen from the following statement :—The authorized force of the Quartermaster General for the fiscal year 1884–85 was 203. This has been *reduced* for the present fiscal year to 123, showing a saving of 80 employees. The appropriation for the first term was, $240,490.00 and for the present year $156,440.00, showing a reduction of $84,055.00, and additional evidence of the economy and good work of the present Administration.

The work of the record and pension division of the Surgeon-General's Office has also been much improved, and is now in a satisfactory condition. It had so far fallen in arrears that 9,511 unanswered calls from the Commissioner of Pensions for information relative to pension claims had accumulated in this office on December 13, 1886. Prior to that date a large number of cases were subjected to a delay of two and one-half and three months, and often for a longer period. This state of affairs had been brought about by a combination of causes, the most important of which were defective methods of work, laxity of discipline, indifference and lack of interest on the part of some of the clerks, many of whom were inattentive to duty, inefficient, physically or mentally disabled, or otherwise incompetent. A belief seemed to pervade the whole office that no improvement in the old system was either desirable or possible, and that any change made in it must necessarily be for the worse. To such an extent was this carried that the two principal officers responsible for this division were of opinion that for efficient and constant work it was necessary to have from two to ten thousand cases always on hand.

Repeated efforts by the Department to secure greater expedition having failed, the methods of work were changed, at once increasing its volume without diminishing its accuracy; the discipline of the force was improved; disabled clerks, who, for various reasons, were entitled to consideration, were assigned to such duties as they could efficiently perform with comfort to themselves; twenty clerks discharged; and it is now generally understood that the work of the office is of the first importance, to which personal preference and convenience must yield, and it has been clearly demonstrated that a large number of cases on hand is not essential to the efficient and economical employment of the clerks engaged on pension work. Any call for information from the records of the Surgeon-General's Office relative to pension claims can now be answered in from one to three days from the date of its receipt.

Since the accession of Mr. Endicott, Congress has passed more so-called "bridge acts," authorizing the construction of bridges across the navigable waters of the United States, than have been passed by Congress under the administration of any Secretary for the previous ten years. A great many of these acts related to bridges across the more important navigable streams of the country, and in nearly every instance legal questions were involved that required the abilities of a very able lawyer to decide. Among the more important of the bridge acts mentioned were those authorizing the construction of the bridge across the Kill von Kull, or Staten Island bridge; the bridge across the Hudson River at Poughkeepsie; and the bridge across the Ohio River at Cincinnati. In each of these acts legal questions arose, which required much deliberation, and Mr. Endicott was enabled, through his intelligence and acumen, to render such decisions as would prove not to be inimical to the interests of the United States, at the same time observing all the principles of equity and justice to the corporations building these bridges.

When Mr. Endicott became Secretary of War, he found great inequality in the punishment of soldiers for similar offences in the different departments and divisions of the Army. With a view to correcting the injustice done to many by the action of courts, he caused the code of military law known as the Articles of War to be examined, looking to their amendment so as to make them more in consonance with the spirit of the age in which we live than at the time of their original adoption, nearly a hundred years ago. He recommended to Congress that specific punishments should be awarded for particular offences, and not to leave to courts-martial the discretion given them in the Articles of War as they stand to-day. In the meantime, to do what he could within the law, he determined to make more uniform the punishments awarded for desertion, by fixing the period of confinement at two years, for in different departments and divisions they would be sentenced from three to four or five years' confinement for this offence, while in a very few instances some courts would sentence them to two years. Believing that the sentences for these long periods were oppressive, the Secretary of War limited the period of confinement in the military prisons, if the person's behavior was such as to enable him to do so, to two years.

In matters of administration few men who have had the experience of Mr. Endicott have done more to simplify the duties of the Department, and to inaugurate economy in the discharge of its functions. Wherever it was possible to reduce expenses without crippling the service to any extent, the Secretary has retrenched the expenses of the Department. Probably never in the administration of the affairs of the War Department have the requirements of the law been so carefully observed as since his advent as head of the Department.

CHAPTER VIII.

THE NAVY DEPARTMENT.

THE Secretary of the Navy performs such duties as the President of the United States, who is Commander-in-Chief, may assign him, and has the general superintendence of construction, manning, armament, equipment, and employment of vessels of war.

THE SECRETARY OF THE NAVY.

WILLIAM C. WHITNEY

Was born at Conway, Mass., July 15, 1841. After graduating from Williston Seminary at Easthampton, Mass., he entered Yale College in 1859; from there he entered the law school of Harvard College, from which he graduated in 1865. He continued the study of law in the office of Hon. Abraham R. Lawrence, in New York City, was admitted to the bar, and entered upon the practice of law in New York. In 1872 he was appointed inspector of schools in the same city, and in August, 1875, was appointed corporation counsel. This was at the time of the downfall of the Tweed ring. The position had amounted to little for many years; but now it suddenly became important, partly because of the mass of litigation over fraudulent claims against the city, but largely through the celerity, energy, and ability shown by Mr. Whitney in clearing off the cases. This achievement established his reputation as a lawyer, and he maintained it during his continuance in office, which he subsequently resigned.

Mr. Whitney is a natural born organizer, and in his management of the New York County Democracy proved his ability in promoting measures for definite objects. As Secretary of the Navy, Mr. Whitney has had the good-will and support of universal public opinion in his efforts to secure a first-class navy for the United States; and we now propose to show what has been done by the Navy Department under his control.

Under the present Secretary, a great advance has been made in the work of this department. An entire plant for a new navy has been laid, and the work is steadily progressing towards a successful termination. One great reason for this success is the determination of the Secretary to have this department managed upon business principles, without regard to the red-tape routine which existed on his taking command. As is well known, the condition of our navy in 1883 was any thing but satisfactory, and proper credit should be given to Secretary Whitney for placing this country in a position where we shall soon be free from any danger from a foreign foe.

The striking features of the present administration of the Navy Department have been,—

1st, The high character of its designs for warships; the great advance in these beyond the point reached in the designs for the "Chicago," "Atlanta," "Boston," and "Dolphin" (in 1883); and the methods of making contracts for the construction of new vessels, whereby all competitors are fully acquainted with the definite plans and details of the vessels before bidding, and contractors are rewarded for an excess of performance beyond that specified and required, or are fined for a failure to comply with the requirements.

NAME.	Displacement.	Trial Speed.	Horse-Power.	Horse-Power per Ton of Machinery.	Built at.	Date of Contract.
CHICAGO	4,500	16.3	5,084	5.4	Chester	1883
ATLANTA	3,190	15.5	3,350	5.1	Chester	1883
BOSTON	3,190	14.9	3,780	5.7	Chester	1883
DOLPHIN	1,485	15.5	2,253	5.6	Chester	1883
		Estimated.				
BALTIMORE	4,413	19 to 20	10,700	11.9	Philadelphia	1886
CHARLESTON	3,730	18 to 19	7,500	10.5	San Francisco	1886
YORKTOWN	1,700	16.0	3,500	10.3	Philadelphia	1886
PETREL	890	13.0	1,300	10.0	Baltimore	1886
BENNINGTON	1,700	16.0	3,500	10.3	Chester	1887
CONCORD	1,700	16.0	3,500	10.3	Chester	1887
NEWARK	4,083	18.0	8,500	10.1	Philadelphia	1887
PHILADELPHIA	4,324	19 to 20	10,700	12.2	Philadelphia	1887
SAN FRANCISCO	4,083	19 to 20	10,700	12.2	San Francisco	1887
VESUVIUS	800	20 to 21	4,000	16.0	Philadelphia	1887
TORPEDO BOAT	99	23.0	1,600	34.0	Bristol, R.I.	1888
	Armored Vessels.					
MAINE	6,648	17.0	9,000	9.9	New York Navy Yard,	1887
TEXAS	6,300	17.0	8,600	10.4	New York Navy Yard,	1887

An examination of the appended table will show the progress made in the requirements for speed, horse-power, and reduced weight of machinery, the amount of work performed or in hand, and the wider distribution of naval ship-building throughout the country.

2d, Furnishing the means to induce the establishment of plant and facilities for the manufacture of gun-forgings, armor, and heavy shafting, within the United States, so as to enable the Government and private firms to be independent of foreign manufacturers; and the creation of naval gun factories at the Washington Navy Yard and elsewhere.

Hitherto, it has been necessary to purchase heavy steel shaftings, armor-plates, and steel forgings for guns of more than eight-inch calibre, abroad; but under the contract of the Navy Department with the Bethlehem Iron Company, the forgings of guns up to twelve-inch calibre will begin to be delivered in August; the shafting for new vessels can be made at same time; and steel armor plates, ranging in thickness from three to twelve inches, will be delivered in 1889; while the gun factory will at the same time be in position to build the highest power guns up to sixteen inches calibre. (At the present time it can and has built ten-inch guns.)

Heretofore it has been necessary to buy heavy steel shafting abroad: hereafter it can be furnished within the United States.

In addition to the more powerful and heavier guns to be built at the naval gun factory, the Navy Department will be supplied with the recently developed rapid-fire guns, with which all navies are arming, by the firm of Hotchkiss & Co., which has established connections in Connecticut for the manufacture of their guns and ammunition, all of which will be of domestic material and workmanship.

The enormous benefit to be derived by the country, in the possession of the means and increased facilities for arming its fleet or other fortifications, cannot be overestimated.

3*d*, The improvement in the system of purchases, care of stores, etc.

By the consolidation of all naval stores under one store keeper at each naval station, great economy has been accomplished. The reduction during the first year under this system, in the expense of handling and caring for stores, including clerks, has been over 25 per cent, or a net gain of over $55,000.

The saving to the Government through the improved methods of making contracts for the entire naval service, and of concentrating these under one head, has been very great.

With reference to the former and the present systems of making purchases by contract and in open market for the navy, it is difficult to present a comparative statement of results, or an exact showing of economy now achieved, owing to the lack of data at command concerning the former method. Under that method, each bureau controlled its own purchases; making them at such times and in such manner, under the law, as each saw fit to select. In order to exhibit a comprehensive statement of the results achieved through that system, exhaustive and lengthy research would be needed in the respective bureaus.

But with regard to the present system, it may be said that the Government secures much better terms by buying as much as possible under yearly contracts, thereby aggregating the purchase of similar supplies for the various stations in one or more contracts made at one time. By consolidating the work of purchase as far as possible, there must also be a large reduction in the expense of advertising.

The annual contracts, ninety-three in number, made with this bureau for the present fiscal year, 1887–88, amounted to $548,398.86; the open purchases in pursuance of approved requisitions upon the purchasing bureau amount, for the first ten months of the year, to $332,616.82. These figures embrace the general purchases, under contract or in open market, pertaining to all the bureaus except provisions and clothing and medicine and surgery, and also coal and stationery for these two bureaus.

For the ensuing fiscal year all the work of contracts and open purchase, and all the accounts and returns, will be based upon the new classified schedule of naval supplies and material. By the system adopted, the purchasing bureau will be able to report at the end of the year the exact value under each of the classes of the schedule of receipts, expenditures, and balances remaining in hand at every station and on board every ship. These results can be presented in tabulated form in such manner as to give a valuable digest of the year's work in all that relates to the purchase and expenditure of naval supplies.

It will thus be seen that in the Navy Department, as in all other departments of this Administration, there is a steady advance in satisfactory results, which are secured at an economical saving to the finances of the nation.

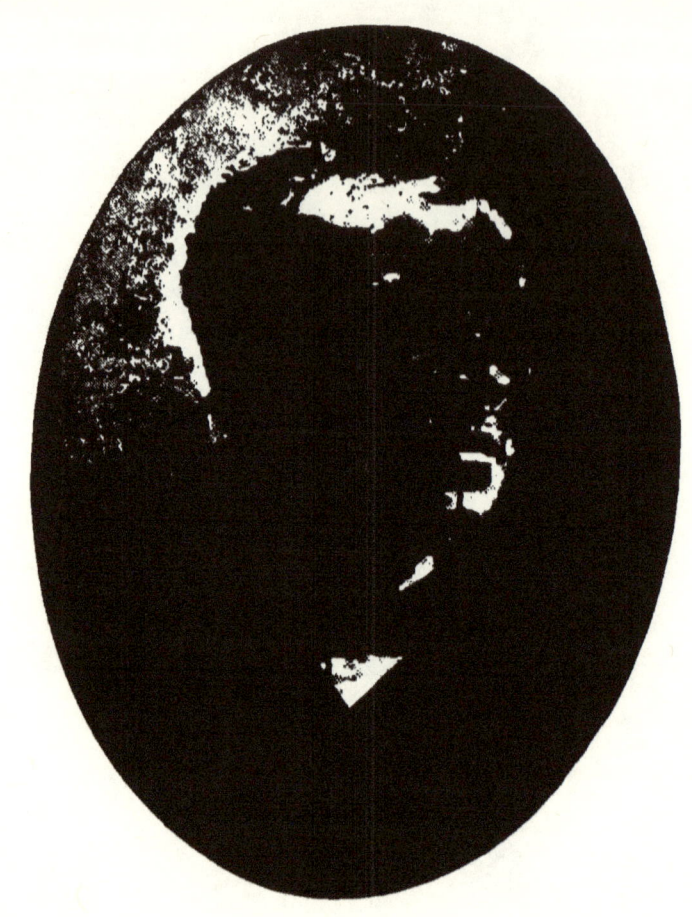

CHAPTER IX.

THE POST-OFFICE DEPARTMENT.

The Postmaster-General has the direction and management of the Post-Office Department. He appoints all officers and employees of the Department, except the three Assistant Postmasters-General, who are appointed by the President, by and with the advice and consent of the Senate; appoints all postmasters whose compensation does not exceed one thousand dollars; makes postal treaties with foreign Governments, by and with the advice and consent of the President, awards and executes contracts, and directs the management of the domestic and foreign mail service.

THE POSTMASTER-GENERAL.
DON M. DICKINSON.

Was born in Auburn, New York State, about 1846, and is therefore forty-two years old. His family came from the State of Massachusetts, where it was widely extended and well known. His father, Asa Dickinson, settled in Michigan when Don was a boy, and he was educated in that State, obtaining the degree of Bachelor of Laws in 1869.

Mr. Dickinson early showed great capacity as a civil lawyer, and as a business man's attorney he is said to have no superior in his State.

His professional prosperity has kept pace with the rise in his reputation, his income for several years having been not less than $25,000. Mr. Dickinson has not until very recently been prominent in politics, his interests as well as his energies having been engrossed by his profession.

In 1872, being still a young man, he advocated the election of Greely; in 1876, he was Chairman of the State Committee of the Democratic party; in 1884, he was a member of the National Committee which managed the Democratic canvass, and December 6th, 1887, he was nominated by the President as Postmaster-General.

There is no Department in the Government that appeals to the interest of every American citizen so strongly as the Post-Office Department. Its agents are welcomed from the Atlantic to the Pacific, from the mountains of Alaska to the plains of Texas, and probably few of our readers, when in daily receipt of their correspondence, have the faintest idea of the enormous extent of the duties so ably managed by this Department under the careful supervision of the Postmaster-General, from whose last report we annex such extracts as will in a condensed form supply such information as may be most interesting.

> The expectation of growth and improvement in the affairs of the postal service, indulged in previous reports, has been realized during the past year. In part arising from an extension of the limits of mailable matter of the fourth class—ordered to meet the requirements of trade—and from the receipts of the special-delivery service, but chiefly from the greater employment of all

postal facilities consequent upon the rising business prosperity of the country, faithfully reflected in the postal service, the revenues have gained upon the preceding year by nearly $4,840,000, attaining a height never reached before, despite the restrictive operations of various reductions in the rates of postage. Upon the other hand, the study of economy has not been without effect in restraining the necessarily rising scale of expenditure, so that the increase of cash disbursements has but little overstepped $2,000,000. * * * The time is probably not distant when, if the wisest measures of economy be pursued, the rate of charge upon letters can be properly lowered to one cent an ounce, and some diminishment permitted in the postages upon merchandise and other matter. But the letter postage of the United States is now fixed at a rate below that of all other countries save one, and, when the distances of transportation are considered, is cheaper than in any other, and the combined receipts from all mail matter not of the first class fall far short of its handling, affording little claim therefore for less postage charges.

The paramount duty of the Government, so far as it concerns this Department, is to furnish the most perfect and useful postal facilities to the people, within the authority of the Constitution, which the skill of man can provide. It is due to the character of the citizens of this country, to their freedom and enlightenment, to their enterprise and activity, to their wealth and power, and especially to the intimacy of their personal relations maintained over so great an expanse of territory to an extent never equalled, hardly aimed at, elsewhere on the globe, from which arise the fraternity of feeling and community of interest that furnish the safest guarantees for the future stability and value of our Federal institutions. It is, indeed, their due as a personal, individual right, because the Government monopolizes the postal business and forbids them all other attempts at self-service. Upon every ground the postal service rightfully urges a constant and exacting demand upon legislative and executive wisdom and labor for its enlargement and improvement to the utmost of perfectibility. * * *

The whole number of post-offices on the 1st day of October, 1887, had become 55,434, of which 2,381 were salaried or Presidential offices, distributed in classes, and 53,053 were fourth class. Besides these were 625 branch offices or stations, an increase of 12, for the sale of stamps only. Of the whole, 8,089 were money-order offices and 110 money-order stations. * * *

The division of post-offices into the two general classes — by distinguishing those the importance and magnitude of whose business is such as to require independent and separate maintenance from those which can properly be carried on in connection with a private business — implies that the former be regarded and treated entirely as Government offices in every particular of their affairs. This consequence is demanded by the soundest principles of public business, and its recognition appears to promise far more satisfactory and efficient service. The office should then become the care of the Department, be provided and equipped, supplied and maintained at its cost, and the postmaster paid by a salary measured by the nature of the responsibilities and duties imposed upon him. His time and labor, reasonably exacted, belong then to the Government, to be applied not only to proper supervision but to such other duties of his office as their use may enable the proper discharge of by him personally; and for the excess of necessary service required the proper provision of clerks devolves upon the Department.

The Postmaster-General makes the following important statement in reference to the cost of the Post-Office Buildings.

Obviously the first objection to be fairly met and perfectly guarded is the risk of unnecessary and lavish expenditure; and the sure economy of such a course of extensive construction demands to be demonstrated and its satisfactory safeguards discerned and provided. Yet it will be remarked that Congress necessarily loses no control over the subject, and can apply any checks from time to time not foreseen to be requisite but discovered to be by trial; and the official responsibility of the officers of the Department, with the limitations fixed by appropriation and by public criticism, affords trustworthy grounds for confidence in the experiment. Indeed it may be truly said, notwithstanding instances of peculation and criminal misconduct inseparable from human trusts, that the record of the vast expenditures and performances of the Post-Office Department, during its history, displays such fidelity in the use of public money and the accomplishment of results so satisfactorily answerable to its proportionable outlays, that no agency of the Government promises to better justify the proper deposit of extensive authority to attempt a great undertaking for the public benefit and the improvement of its service.

In reference to Post-Office clerks the report of the Postmaster-General makes the following suggestions which convey conviction to the practical mind of every business man.

The first aim should seemingly be to settle the rules by which to determine in what offices and to what extent clerical service, in addition to the postmaster's personal service, ought to be furnished by the Department. This is properly dependent on the nature and magnitude of the work required at the office. It does not depend on the gross receipts, nor is it to be gauged by them. The tables show this clearly. And the work in post-offices divides into many different kinds, each of which requires an especial consideration. The desideratum is, a fixed scale for measurement — not in money, but in clerical power or capacity — of the several kinds of work, in order to make the adequate provision for each branch of duty, and in total. This appears attainable by a study of each species of labor sufficiently to determine how much of it a person of average competency should perform in a given time; the perception of the proper unit of measure in each grade of duty.

Given the rules, the particular facts to which they are to be applied must then be reliably found. This suggests the second aim of such an inquiry: the discovery or invention of the methods by which the postmaster may trustworthily take the census of his various duties and make faithful reports thereof in such form that the true estimation of the clerical service due his circumstances arises from the application of the rules.

The third point indicated is, that the entire body of post-office clerks requires to be intelligently graded into classes and divisions, adapted to the work in post-offices, the pay of each grade and rank predetermined; and assignment of the force found necessary for the work — according to the prescribed rules — should be of clerks of the requisite grades, chargeable to the Department, instead of being in money to the postmaster to employ service. * * *

So signally helpful to the public service is a well-trained, well-disposed, faithful, honest, and patriotic postal clerk, who is devoted to his duty, and content to confine himself to its excellent performance as his best recommendation, eschewing foreign contentions which excite needless animosity and invite attack, that no superior who sustains the care of the service fails to recognize the injury to the public interests of his loss. It is undeniably true that equally as good may elsewhere be found, and in time a practised and competent successor may stand in his stead. But it is not enough for the particular exigency that humanity betters with time, and the present and future hold as suitable for every vocation as the past. Time is of the essence of excellence in the mail service, and immediate provision for a loss is its imperative demand, rendering the needless loss of a valuable, well-governed employé in such a place a breach of public duty. The private wrong may be also great, especially when many years have been given to faithful service of the Government for a rate of pay which offers no possibility of much saving, and natural disqualification for other avocations can not but have resulted.

The postal service is prominent among the agencies which the common Government can better wield for the common good than any private or corporate hands. Yet its efficiency demands so vast a body of public servants, responsive to the will of the central authority, that no branch is more within the just apprehension of lodging excessive power in the Federal Government. No principle has been more aptly and vigorously invoked to limit the extension of the Department's powers, especially to withhold control over the kindred function adjoined to it by so many civilized countries, the management of correspondence by the electric wire. Yet no counteracting force can more effectively modify the danger and deliver the agency of Government from the chains of that wise fear to a greater public usefulness than such a course of appointment and such a tenure in appointees as will render them dependent only on excellence in public service and fidelity to the common interest, while they remain in and subject to the influences of different localities to which they belong and their service is immediately directed. Discrimination in original selection diminishes the risks of incurring the censure of sound discipline; and amenability to no other criticism for continuance in duty enfranchises the officer in great degree from the perilous subserviency.

The importance of the CARRIER SERVICE is recognized.

There should be no hesitation in providing every city and town in the United States with this service, whose business interests and local conditions are such as to make it of an advantage compensatory to its cost. There can justly be no shorter limitation. One such community of our people is equally entitled with another; and all such are entitled by the best claim, American citizenship upon American enterprise, to the highest conveniences of the best postal system. No limitation is to be justly found in the relation of local postage to the cost of this service. The aggregate of such postage exceeded the entire cost of carrier-delivery in the past year by $2,072,561.62, and each year the excess will be more. But 30 cities out of 329 now in possession realized this result independently, so that the claim of such as do not enjoy it is equal to that of the other 299 which are assisted to maintain it. The liberal policy approved by Congress is fully warranted by the finances of the postal service, and will doubtless be generously pursued hereafter. * * *

The extent of our DOMESTIC SERVICE is given: —

The large area of our country and the equality of privileges enjoyed in all parts of it, with the corresponding diffusion of all the advantages, accompanied by all the demands of high civilization, have caused the gradual augmentation of our system of mail transportation to its present immensity, and continually press its greater extension. The most trustworthy statistics at command show that all the residue of the globe possesses no more miles of railroads employed in mail carriage than the United States alone, and that no other one nation maintains one-quarter the amount of other methods of mail transportation. * * *

In 1886 there were handled by clerks in the Railway Mail Service, of letters, ordinary mail matter, registered packages, through registered pouches, and inner registered sacks, 5,345,846,044. In 1887, 5,851,394,057; being an increase of 505,148,053 pieces, or 9.46 per cent.

And the extent of FOREIGN SERVICE as follows: —

The Foreign Mail Service has been satisfactorily conducted during the past year. The use of all vessels, whether foreign or domestic, departing from our ports for other countries, has been regularly tendered to the Department, and the most favorable opportunities for frequent and rapid transportation afforded by ocean carriers have been availed of. In the transatlantic service, where many vessels of rival lines compete for patronage, the swiftest have been chosen for employment from week to week in accordance with the settled policy of the Department. The service so secured is unequalled by that of any other country; contrasting conspicuously to our advantage with the service inward from Great Britain, which is maintained at greater cost and less efficiency by adherence to the system of contracting with particular lines for annual subsidies. The rates paid by the United States are highly remunerative to the principal companies whose swift ships secure the heaviest mails; probably yielding greater profit, proportioned to space, weight, and expense, than anything transported except jewels and precious metals; if, indeed, they are to be excepted.

The entire weight of our foreign mail despatches by sea was nearly 1,500,000 kilograms, or 3,278,269 pounds, of which 568,728 were of letter mail and 2,709,541 pounds of prints and merchandise samples. Nine-tenths of the letter mail was European-bound, and but about one-tenth for South America, the West Indies, Pacific Islands, and the Orient combined; but of the paper and samples mail the latter countries received nearly one-fourth, and the despatches across the Atlantic were little over three-fourths.

The increase in the gross weight of our ocean mails was about 410,488 pounds; the transatlantic letter mail gaining 10.59 per cent. and the Central and South American 19.21 per cent.; the paper mail in approximate similar ratios. As an indication of increasing trade with the countries of our hemisphere these are acceptable facts. The increase in the sailings from our ports of steamships bound for the West Indies, Central or South American ports is pleasingly cumulative, having been greater during the last fiscal year than for many previous years, perhaps than for any, the total number of such sailings at the three ports of New York, New Orleans, and San Francisco being reported at 831, as against 712 during the preceding year.

The following important Postal Conventions have been executed since March 4, 1885, with Tasmania, Mexico and Canada, also Parcel Post Conventions with Jamaica, Barbadoes, the Bahamas and British Honduras, and nearly completed with Mexico; through these conventions our citizens enjoy advantages which when understood will be sure to be appreciated.

Besides the foregoing, negotiations have been opened with the countries of the Central and South American states, and the favorable replies received indicate that, after a sufficient consideration, many, if not all, will join in this arrangement of such excellent promise to enlarge the commercial and individual intercourse between the peoples of this continent. It is the purpose of this Department to spare no pains to this end, if the course shall be found to have the favor of Congress.

The great gain which would surely follow such a system with the Republics of Uruguay and the Argentine Confederation furnish additional reasons for the provision of a direct mail between those countries and ours.

The natural ending of the Post-Office Department is

THE DEAD-LETTER OFFICE.

The Dead-Letter Office was placed under charge of a superintendent at the beginning of the year, as a separate office, pursuant to the Act of Congress authorizing its detachment from the office of the Third Assistant. From the report of the Superintendent it appears that the work of this office has considerably increased.

During the year 5,578,965 pieces of mail matter were treated, increasing by 11.4 per cent. over 1886 and by about 17 per cent. over 1885. This increase is in part attributable to the enlarged volume of mail matter transported, and partly to the greater care taken by postmasters in rendering returns of undelivered matter and withdrawing from the mails such as is unmailable.

Among the interesting items of the work performed it is to be noted that 456,183 pieces of mail arriving from foreign lands were returned to the country of origin; that 12,725 letters, inclosing in the aggregate $22,639.12, and 21,868 letters containing drafts, notes, checks, money-orders, etc., of the amount in face value of $7,581,761.10, were restored to the owners.

There was derived to the postal revenue from dead mail matter the sum of $9,593.77, $714.48 in excess of the previous year.

Magazines, pamphlets, and other reading matter incapable of return, have been distributed to the various charitable institutions in the District of Columbia, in all 18,182 pieces.

In closing this most interesting summary of the work of the Post-Office Department it will be remembered that it was first under the administration of Colonel Vilas, now Secretary of the Interior Department, and that Mr. Dickinson has entered with energy upon the work so well started. The present Postmaster-General is the author of the very important bill now before Congress to provide separate small post-offices throughout the country at an actual saving to the Government and conferring a benefit upon our people which is sure to be appreciated. In no way could we have presented more clearly to our readers the progress made by the various Departments under the present administration than by thus showing that the Post-Office Department has accomplished more work at less cost and to the better satisfaction of the entire nation than has ever been done before.

CHAPTER X.

THE DEPARTMENT OF THE INTERIOR.

The Secretary of the Interior is charged with the supervision of public business relating to patents for inventions; pension and bounty lands; the public lands, including mines; the Indians; education; railroads; the public surveys; the census, when directed by law; the custody and distribution of public documents; and certain hospitals and eleemosynary institutions in the District of Columbia. He also exercises certain powers and duties in relation to the Territories of the United States.

THE SECRETARY OF THE INTERIOR.

WILLIAM F. VILAS

was born at Chelsea, Vt., July 9, 1840. He removed with his parents, in 1851, to Madison, Wis., graduated from the Wisconsin State University in 1858, and from the law school, Albany, N.Y., in 1860, when he was admitted to the Wisconsin bar, and entered upon the practice of the law at Madison. In 1862 Mr. Vilas raised a company of volunteers, and joined the Twenty-third Wisconsin Regiment as captain in March, 1863; was promoted to lieutenant-colonel, and had command of his regiment during the siege of Vicksburg and for two months afterwards. Resigned his commission in 1863, and renewed the practice of his profession at Madison. He was appointed lecturer in the Department of Law, Wisconsin State University, and was a member of the Board of Regents of that institution, from 1875 to 1878.

By appointment of the Supreme Court of the State of Wisconsin, Col. Vilas was one of the revisers of the statutes of the State.

In 1884 he was chairman of the Democratic National Committee. It has been generally conceded at home that Col. Vilas was the leader of the Madison bar, and he was recognized as one of the most able and eloquent advocates of Wisconsin. His reputation as an orator began with his famous eulogy of Grant at the Chicago banquet. Col. Vilas is a man of genuine brilliancy, and of great abilities as a lawyer and a scholar, and his selection by President Cleveland as Postmaster-General was universally applauded. Upon the selection of Secretary Lamar to fill a seat on the supreme bench, Mr. Cleveland appointed Col. Vilas Secretary of the Interior. He has entered upon his duties with his usual conscientious energy, and the large portion of our people who are interested in the work of the Interior Department can form their conclusions as to its progress from the statements which follow.

The work of this department comprises the most important interests of the country, and it is quite impossible to do more than refer to such offices and bureaus as have charge of the leading subjects to which attention should be called.

THE PATENT OFFICE.

In this important bureau of the Interior Department, as in the other departments of the Government, we see the same salutary reforms and changes which have characterized the advent of the present Administration.

The country was met with what seemed to be a very plausible and vehement objection at first, that a change of administration would work disastrously to the business of the departments and bureaus. It was charged that turning out old and trusted officials, and putting in new ones, would have the effect of impairing the public service.

Time has contradicted these misgivings and forebodings, that a change would impair the public service; and it is confidently claimed that in no bureau has such a charge been more plainly and clearly contradicted, than in the Patent Office. Not only has the public business of this office not been in the least lessened, or the efficiency of the public service impaired, but, on the other hand, we see a steady growth, both of the business of the office, and the respect in which it is held by the inventors of the country; and that this steady growth, this keeping up in its full vigor the business of the office, has been accomplished under many disadvantageous circumstances.

During President Cleveland's administration, the records as seen from time to time in the reports of both the Hon. M. V. Montgomery, the first Commissioner of Patents under President Cleveland's administration, and the Hon. Benton J. Hall, the present incumbent, give a most satisfactory and creditable showing of the condition of affairs in the Patent Office.

Mr. Montgomery succeeded Hon. Benjamin Butterworth; and it will be seen, that, with about the same force, and lessened expenditure, more business was transacted from 1885 up to the end of his official incumbency than was ever before transacted in the same time in the history of the Patent Office. It will also be seen, from his annual report to Congress, that the number of applications, and the number of patents granted, was largely in excess of applications received and patents granted by his predecessor; and that he transacted a larger amount of business, and turned into the treasury over fifty-seven thousand dollars more than was turned in by the preceding Commissioner of Patents.

It should also be noted, that, for the first six months of the fiscal year of 1886, the Commissioner of Patents covered into the United States Treasury $114,899.74, which was a greater surplus for six months than for the entire year of 1884, and that the applications for patents exceeded those for the same period by nearly two thousand.

The undisputed concurrent testimony of the officers of the bureau, a large per cent of whom are Republicans holding over from old Republican administrations, shows that the bureau has never before in the history of the office done so much work, at so small an expense, and with the same official and clerical help, as under the administration of the Hon. Benton J. Hall. And it is proper here to say that he has shown rare skill in the management of the Patent Office; and when it is remembered that probably seventy per cent of the officials under him, and upon whom he must rely largely in the direction of the duties pertaining to the office, hold political views different from his own, it is a worthy tribute to his efficiency and sterling executive worth that he should have enlisted the cordial co-operation of this force in the many valuable suggestions and reforms made and inaugurated by himself.

The decisions of this commissioner, by the universal consent of the bar of the district, and by the attorneys practising before the office, representing as they do the interests of the thousands of inventors all over the country, take a high rank. Indeed, so marked has been the judicial ability displayed by Commissioner Hall, that it has drawn from the leading papers of the Republican party many worthy tributes to this efficient and scholarly official. Prominent among the notices in the Republican papers of Mr. Hall's rare efficiency and capacity, is one taken from the " New York Tribune " of Oct. 1, 1887, and voices probably the sentiments of all. This article is printed in the " Scientific American," one of the ablest industrial journals in the world, with added editorial comments of a high character. It says, —

"In brief, he seems to recognize the fact that the Patent Office is not a political office; that it is supported by the men of a particular class, the inventors, — so well supported, in short, that the yearly dividend of twenty per cent is realized from the fees paid in, while there is an accumulated surplus of three millions of dollars in the treasury.

"Every week's issue of the 'Official Gazette' contains from one to three of the commissioner's decisions on points of office practice, designed to bring uniformity in the same among the different divisions. If the story told by the attorneys is to be believed, something of that kind is badly needed."

The "Scientific American" then proceeds to add editorially, —

"The encomium of the 'Tribune' on Commissioner Hall is just, and reminds one of the patent-office administration under the commissionerships of Judge Mason and Judge Holt, which was a good while ago, but whom the few of us live to remember with satisfaction."

In this necessarily brief notice space is not permitted to mention the many able and valuable decisions of Commissioner Hall, touching as they do the direct and varied interests of the tens of thousands of inventors throughout the country. It is a worthy tribute to President Cleveland's selection of this able official to refer in this connection to the many reforms recommended in the Patent Office by Commissioner Hall; foremost of which, and as forming a part of the issues to which the public mind will be directed in the coming campaign, is the abuse of organized wealth and corporate power as they affect the actual workings of the Patent Office which the commissioner has striven to remedy.

Corporate power, grown to an alarming size during the past quarter of a century by special class legislation, and the many privileges given to it during the Republican *régime*, has pushed its baleful influences even into the industrial arts.

For years it has been known that the real inventors of the country, most of them humble but skilled mechanics in the industrial arts, have utterly failed to secure the benefits of their inventive genius. Seldom has it been that the real inventor has reaped the harvest of his patience and his skill. It has been seen that the influence and greed of corporate power, with its restless and corrupting energies, have been specially directed to the monopolization of labor-saving devices in all branches of mechanics; so that it can be said to control, and, in fact, has aggregated to itself by the use of enormous capital, the skill of the inventive genius of the country. Almost every invention, representing years of some ingenious mechanic's life, is immediately seized upon by some monopoly or other, the interest of the inventor bought for a song, and the benefits of the invention, which the spirit of the patent laws intended should go to the public at large, have been held for the advantage of the special few, to be doled out by corporations to the general public at enormous profits to the managers.

The cause of general industry gains nothing. Labor where it has thus been controlled by corporations has received no substantial benefits from invention, and capital organized against the interests of the masses received the enormous gains which have made these monopolies threatening factors in social and political life, inimical to the interests of the masses of the laboring people.

Commissioner Hall, among other valuable suggestions for reform, referring to the corrupt power of corporate wealth, and the pernicious influences of its presence in the Patent Office, said in his annual report for the year ending December, 1887, when the consideration of section 4894 of the Revised Statutes was before him, that this section of the statute enables rich and influential parties to keep the applications for patents, of which they are the assignees, pending in the office for years before their patent is issued. In the mean time, they are engaged in manufacturing and putting upon the market the article or improvement, but warning the public that the patent is "applied for;" the effect of which is to give them the absolute control of the monopoly of the invention, and to deter all other inventors from entering the same field of invention, and manufacturing the same article. The commissioner, seeing the danger which must inevitably result to the inventive talent of the country from this illegitimate use of wealth and corporate power, recommended to Congress that this section should be modified, and that there be vested in the commissioner a discretion to declare any application forfeited for want of prosecution whenever he is satisfied that such should be done. This suggestion promptly acted upon will go far towards checking the domination of capital over the development of the industrial arts. It would be a step in the direction of freeing the laboring classes, out of which comes the inventive skill and genius of a nation, from being the mental slaves of powerful corporations.

The work of the Patent Office for the year 1887 can be best understood from the following detail.

THE DEPARTMENT OF THE INTERIOR. 179

Receipts from	applications	. . .	$1,014,265 00
"	" copies	. . .	83,267 40
"	" deeds	. . .	23,416 70
"	" "Gazette"	. . .	14,402 53
"	" labels	. . .	2,903 50
	Total income	. . .	$1,138,255 13

For the six months ending June 30, 1888, there were received 86,080 letters, containing in money $508,091.26. The whole business of this important office has been conducted with more celerity, less proportional expense, and to the better satisfaction of patentees than ever before; and we may look forward, under another four years of the present Administration, to results which will prove the wisdom of the Executive in managing all departments upon business principles.

THE PENSION BUREAU.

The work of this important bureau is perhaps more closely connected with the hearts and homes of our people than any other. It is a great monument to those who have sacrificed their lives for the liberties of the nation. It represents an act of national justice hitherto unparalleled in the world's history. Through its action the widow and the orphan receive that proper recognition for the services of the husband and father, which a grateful nation will render so long as they live to receive it.

It is a satisfaction to state that under the present administration the work of this bureau has in every respect progressed in such a manner as to win admiration from all those who have any idea of what has been done in the Pension Bureau since March 16, 1885; and a comparison may fairly be challenged in the number of pensions granted, in the large number of veterans who have had their pensions increased, in the extraordinary work of the office, through its Special Examination Division, in making that critical examination of the rights of claimants at their homes and elsewhere all over the country.

Since the present administration of the office up to the 15th day of June, 1888, a period of three years and three months, the enormous number of one hundred and sixty-seven thousand *new names* have been added to the pension rolls of the nation, and more than one hundred and thirty-eight thousand scarred veterans have had their pensions increased. In the rapid movement of events we hardly have time to pause and reflect upon what this indicates; viz., that an army larger than the *combined armies* of Wellington and Napoleon at Waterloo have received through the magnificent liberality of the Government of these United States its generous bounty, and that this large additional amount has been granted under the present administration, thus affording additional proof (if it were needed) that the Democratic party is true to the memory of those who fought their country's battles, true to those who upheld the old flag in the fiery storm of war.

It must be borne in mind, that, with these gratifying results and this greatly increased work, the clerical force of the Bureau of Pensions remains *the same* as it was at the commencement of the present Administration.

CIVIL SERVICE.

The whole force is subject to the rules and regulations governing the civil service. No appointments are made, nor have any been made, in this bureau except through the avenue of civil service examinations and certification. At the time the present Commissioner of Pensions assumed charge of the bureau, he found *ninety-five* per cent of this clerical force selected from that political party antagonistic to the present Administration, nearly all of whom were appointed regardless of civil service qualifications. New appointments, however, have been made only through the channel of civil service examination, and with most gratifying results; and of the original ninety-five per cent, it is safe to assert that at least seventy-five per cent still remain undisturbed at their desks. *No discharges* have been made except in cases of gross inefficiency, neglect of duty, or evidences of partisanship incompatible with the efficient administration of the office. The Pension Bureau during the current year will distribute the immense sum of eighty millions of the people's money, payable to over four hundred and sixteen thousand pensioners. This great work will be accomplished at far less expense than ever before; for the reason that in this bureau, as in all others under the present Administration, the work is being done for the first time upon *business principles*, thus securing a larger amount of labor upon a more economic and satisfactory basis. In this connection it is but just to allude to the attempts made by *pension sharks* to introduce fraudulent claims; thus not only doing injury to those who are justly entitled to their country's bounty, but at the same time casting a stigma upon the fair name of the nation. To every sensible man or woman who reads this article, the action of the President in putting his veto upon all such attempts to defraud the Government and the people can admit of but one construction; viz., that in Grover Cleveland we have secured a President who devotes himself steadily to but one object, and that is the good of this nation, and to prove to his fellow-citizens that " a public office is a public trust."

THE GENERAL LAND-OFFICE.

The Commissioner of Public Lands is charged with the survey, management, and sale of the public domain, and the issuing of titles therefor, whether derived from confirmations of grants made by former governments, by sales, donations, or grants for schools, railroads, military bounties, or public improvements. He is aided by an assistant commissioner. The Land-Office audits its own accounts.

The great importance of this bureau in its relation to the progress of our country cannot be overestimated. Its energies have been devoted, during the present administration, to remedy defects and correct abuses in the public land service. The results of these efforts are so largely in the nature of reforms in the processes and methods of our land system as to prevent adequate estimate; but it appears, from the latest official statement, that there has been secured and restored to the public domain, and recommended for recovery, from March 4, 1885, to May 12, 1888, as follows: —

Total actually restored to the public domain, and opened to entry and settlement, 80,690,720 acres. It must be borne in mind that these lands are secured from railroad forfeitures, indemnity lands, illegal land claims, and withdrawn lands restored; thus offering to the farmer and emigrant an opportunity to secure a comfortable home, and at the same time adding to our national territory an extent of valuable property which would otherwise have been controlled by trusts, syndicates, or corporations. In addition to this great work, there has been accomplished also an examination of other lands, which will fall under the same rules, and which will restore an additional extent of territory, amounting to 65,020,538 acres. This immense territory, comprising lands most favorable for settlement, can accommodate all the emigrants which are likely to arrive in this country within the next twenty years; and we may look forward to another advance in civilization. through farms, villages, towns, and cities, secured by the work of the Land-Office under the present Administration, and at a less proportionate cost than under any previous Administration since the commencement of our government.

INDIAN OFFICE.

The important question of the management of our Indians is one that has given much trouble and embarrassment to this department. The expenses attending such management have been very great, and yet the ultimate results have been so unsatisfactory as to occasion much public and private comment. Following out the suggestions of the President in his annual message, the work of the Indian office has been more carefully attended to under this Administration, and with the result that the condition of our Indian population, and the progress of the work for their enlightenment, is a gratifying and hopeful one. And when it is understood that this has been accomplished at a saving to the nation in the estimates for the year of over four hundred thousand dollars, our fellow-citizens will certainly appreciate the steady and unwearied efforts of the present Administration to carry on its work upon a business basis.

In addition to the above, the Department of the Interior has control of the management of such railroads as are in whole or in part west, north, or south of the Missouri River, and to which the United States have granted any loan of credit or subsidy in lands or bonds. Also it has charge of the Geological Survey, comprising the classification of the public lands, and examination of the geological structure, mineral resources, and products of the national domain; and finally this department has charge of the supervision of the census of the United States, which is taken every tenth year, and the subsequent arrangement, compilation, and publication of the statistics collected. It is a gratifying statement, that, under the present Administration, the immense labor connected with this department has been faithfully conducted at less proportionate expense than ever before, and with results which are universally admitted to be far more satisfactory than could have been expected in so short a time. With another four years of the same capable management, we may look forward to results of even greater importance.

THE BUREAU OF EDUCATION.

The names of Horace Mann, Henry Barnard, and John Eaton are substantial guarantees that the subject of education, in its connection with the present and future welfare of the growing youth of the nation, has been well cared for. In Col. N. H. R. Dawson, the present commissioner, and his able corps of assistants, we have every reason to look forward to a continuation of the good work so well begun. As may be clearly understood from the peculiar and special character of the work of this office, its employés have always been selected specially with reference to their qualifications and intelligence, and possibly to a greater extent than has prevailed in the general clerical service of the government. The late commissioner, Gen. Eaton, was in control of this bureau for sixteen years, and his careful selection of his subordinates, and their retention in office by his successor, under the rules of merit service, has secured the best work being accomplished with the limited force in hand. The special object of this bureau is to inform the public as to the advancement of education in the United States, and this is done through an annual report, which contains all data up to the time of issue. This annual report comprises the general statistics as regards education in the United States, including State school systems with all the facts as to population and percentage of school attendance, which have shown a most gratifying steady increase from year to year; statistics regarding teachers and their salaries in different States; the various State laws relative to education, with public-school receipts and expenditures, are also fully given in detail. The city school systems are then taken up, and the most complete and reliable information supplied upon this important subject. The training of teachers, normal schools, kindergartens, superior instruction of women, statistics regarding colleges, universities, schools of science, and technological schools, all receive due attention. A separate chapter is devoted to professional instruction, comprising all information regarding schools of theology, law, medicine, dentistry, and pharmacy, and a statistical summary of all degrees conferred. The subject of special training comprises much of interest, taking in as it does all that relates to industrial and manual training-schools, military schools, commercial and business colleges, together with training-schools for nurses. Upon the education of special classes full reports will be found supplying interesting statistics connected with the deaf and dumb, blind, feeble-minded, and juvenile delinquents; also, the education of the colored race and that of the Indian. These reports are supplied freely to the public, and should be secured by all interested. They will be found of special value as works of reference in our city, town, and village libraries. A very interesting statement bearing upon foreign education is included, and also a report upon the success in the attempts to introduce education among the Indians in Alaska, which far-off section of our great country is in the special charge of the Bureau of Education. Under the present commissioner all these reports have been brought forward and published up to the latest date possible, and our readers will find in this collection a vast amount of interesting information. Several very important and special pamphlets have also been prepared and published by this bureau, viz.: Proceedings of the department of superintendence of the National Educational Association, February 2-26, 1886, and of the same association March 15-17, 1887. Many of the papers read at these meetings are of absorbing interest, and we would specially call the attention of our readers to an illustrated article relating to Alaska, and what has been done there in connection with education and civilization. The Educational Bureau has also published a most elaborate and important essay upon "The Study of History in American Colleges and Universities," an interesting account of William and Mary College, of Virginia, and a complete catalogue of all the libraries in the United States. Commissioner Dawson, under instructions from the Interior Department, made a personal visit to Alaska, establishing many schools, and otherwise aiding the efforts of those interested in the civilization of these comparatively new citizens of the United States. He had the good fortune to be present at the new settlement of the native Indians from Metlakahtla, whose fate has attracted so much attention during the past year. It will be remembered that they were so harshly treated under the rules of the British government and the church authorities that Mr. William Duncan, the distinguished English missionary, decided to place them under the protection of the American flag. The following description of the exercises upon the occasion of locating their new home will be found specially interesting.

The day was a perfect one, and the visitors were at once put on shore. A more lovely place than this harbor it is impossible to imagine. It is semi-circular in shape, opening out through a number of small islands to the westward. On the east and north were wild, rugged mountains, coming down to the water's edge, and on the south is a low green shore, skirted by a gravel beach that winds in and out in beautiful curves. The place was entirely uninhabited, except by thirty or forty of the men of Metlakahtla, with their families, who had come on as an advance guard. The remainder, in all about one thousand people, men, women, and children, will come as soon as provision can be made for them and the means of transportation shall arrive.

The exercises were impromptu, and Mr. Duncan first addressed his people in their native tongue. He told them of his trip to the United States, and concluded by introducing Hon. N. H. R. Dawson, the United States Commissioner of Education, then upon an official tour of Alaska, who had kindly consented to make an address upon this occasion. In Mr. Dawson's address, interpreted by Mr. Duncan into the native language, for the benefit of those who did not understand English, they were impressively told of the power and glory of the great American government, under whose protection they were coming, and were assured that when its flag was raised over them they would be protected in their lives and liberties, that their homes and lands would be assured to them, and that their education and welfare would be the cherished care of the great government to which they had intrusted themselves.

He congratulated them upon their advent to American soil, and assured them that they would have the sympathy and protection of the government in their new homes, and that, although the general land laws of the United States were not now in force in the Territory, that they would not be disturbed in the use and possession of any lands upon which they might settle and build houses, but that when those laws were extended over the country they would doubtless be allowed to enter and purchase these lands and hold possession of them in preference to others. In the meantime they would have the same advantages of education open to them which are now extended to all the inhabitants of the Territory. Efforts had been made to impress them with the idea that the American government was unfriendly and would show them no kindness. This impression Mr. Dawson successfully dispelled in his address, which was received with great satisfaction by the Indians. When he concluded, the flags were raised, the ship saluting them as they went up with its battery of one gun. The natives then sang "Rock of Ages," exquisitely, in their native tongue. Rev. Dr. Fraser, of San Francisco, in a touching prayer, then commended the new settlement to the protection of Divine Providence, after which all united in singing old "Coronation." One of the principal chiefs, or selectmen, Daniel Ne-ash-kum-ack-kem, then replied to Mr. Dawson's address in a short speech, as follows: —

"Chiefs, I have a few words of truth to let you know what our hearts are saying. The God of heaven is looking at our doings here to-day. You have stretched out your hands to the Tsein-she-ans. Your act is a Christian act. We have long been knocking at the door of another government for justice, but the door has been closed against us. You have risen up and opened your door to us, and bid us welcome to this beautiful spot, upon which we propose to erect our homes. What can our hearts say to this, but that we are thankful and happy! The work of the Christian is never lost. Your work will not be lost to you. It will live, and you will find it after many days. We are here only a few to-day who have been made happy by your words; but when your words reach all of our people, numbering over a thousand, how much more joy will they occasion! What shall we say further to thank you? We were told that there were no slaves under the flag of England. For a long time our hearts relied on this as the truth. We were content and happy; but we now find that our reliance has been misplaced. These promises have been broken; that nation has set at naught its own laws in its treatment of us, and is dealing with us as with slaves. We come to you for protection and safety. Our hearts, though often troubled, have not fainted. We have trusted in God, and he has helped us. We are now able to sleep in peace. Our confidence is restored. God has given us his strength to reach this place of security and freedom, and we are grateful to him for his mercy and loving kindness. We again salute you from our hearts. I have no more to say."

At the conclusion of this reply, which was delivered in the musical intonations of his native tongue, with a grace and eloquence that did credit to the picturesque forum in which he stood, Dr. Fraser gave the benediction. The passengers and natives then joined in one rousing cheer for the old flag, that must have impressed the Metlakahtlans with the fervor and zeal of American patriotism.

CHAPTER XI.

THE DEPARTMENT OF JUSTICE.

The attorney-general is the head of the Department of Justice, and the chief law officer of the government. He represents the United States in matters involving legal questions; he gives his advice and opinions on questions of law when they are required by the President or by the heads of the other executive departments on questions of law arising upon the administration of their respective departments; he exercises a general superintendence and direction over United States attorneys and marshals in all judicial districts in the States and Territories, and he provides special counsel for the United States whenever required by any department of the government.

THE ATTORNEY-GENERAL.

Augustus H. Garland.

A. H. Garland was born in Tipton Co., Tenn., June 11, 1832. In the following year his parents removed to Arkansas. Mr. Garland graduated at St. Joseph College, Bardstown, Ky., in 1849. He studied law, and after his admission to the bar settled in the practice of his profession at Little Rock, Ark.

He opposed the early movements of the South at the commencement of the civil war, but eventually joined his State, Arkansas, in its connection with the Confederacy, and served in the Confederate congress. At the close of the war, Mr. Garland was chosen United States senator, but was refused admission. After serving as Secretary of State for Arkansas he was elected Governor, in 1874, and in 1876 was elected to represent the same State in the United States Senate for a term of six years, from March, 1877. In 1882 he was reëlected for another term, receiving not only the entire vote of his own party, but also that of the Republicans in the State Legislature, only three votes being cast against him. In March, 1885, he was appointed attorney-general of the United States, and took his seat in the Cabinet of President Cleveland.

Judge Garland, while in the United States Senate, enjoyed the confidence and respect of all his colleagues. He was indefatigable in committee work, and his legal knowledge and judicial impartiality made him one of the strongest and most influential members of the judiciary committee. In debate he has always been a strong, forcible speaker, his notable characteristics being, first, conciseness and perspicuity of statement; second, logical order of argument; and, third, power of condensation,— all qualities specially fitting him to occupy the chair of the Department of Justice, the work of which office is herewith given.

We find on examination that in this department, as in all others, there has been a steady gain and improvement not only in the amount of work done, but also that for the first time laws have been actually put in force under the present administration which have heretofore been allowed to remain dormant. That some idea may be arrived at as regards the importance and extent of this department, extracts are made from the last official report of the attorney-general.

BUSINESS OF THE COURT OF CLAIMS.

Since the last report 449 suits, claiming upward of $4,150,000, have been brought under the ordinary jurisdiction of the court.

The total number of such cases now pending is 1,110, claiming upward of $18,250,000.

Under the act of March 3, 1883, known as the "Bowman act," there have been transmitted to the court, to date, 2,038 cases. The amount claimed cannot be stated, but involves a very large sum.

During the last term 147 of these cases, claiming about $1,260,000, were acted on by the court and reported to Congress. Of this number, 34 cases, aggregating upward of $670,000, were dismissed for want of jurisdiction.

In 63 cases the findings of the court were favorable to claimants, but for reduced amounts.

There are now pending about 1,819 cases, involving, in so far as can be ascertained from the petitions and other papers received, upward of $50,000,000.

Under the same act there have been transmitted by heads of departments, to date, 29 claims, amounting in the aggregate to upward of $4,000,000. One case, claiming $1,226,804.81, with interest, was acted on by the court during the term, and a finding for $249,000 certified to the department transmitting the claim.

Nine cases, claiming about $350,000, are now pending, one of which has been submitted, and is now held under advisement by the court.

There are also pending matters entertained by the court under the provisions of section 2 of said act.

FRENCH SPOLIATIONS.

The petitions filed in French spoliations cases number 5,560, representing 2,386 vessels, and about $30,000,000. Thirteen cases arising upon four vessels were reported by the court, with favorable recommendations, to Congress on December 6, 1886.

Sixty-eight additional cases arising upon 29 vessels have been passed upon by the court in favor of claimants and will be reported to Congress at its next session.

Twelve cases upon 12 vessels have been decided against the claimants; 200 additional are now on trial.

The amount reported in favor of claimants in all the 81 cases passed upon, in the aggregate, is about $425,000, varying in sums from $66.40 to $45,318.66.

The general principles involved in these cases have been fully discussed, and four opinions have been delivered by the court, settling some of the important questions governing them.

The following is a summary of the business of the last term:

CLAIMS AGAINST THE UNITED STATES.

There were brought to trial 314 suits, claiming $18,551,605.58. In 24 of these, claiming $105,595.66, judgment was for defendants.

In 290 suits, claiming $18,446,009.92, judgment was for claimants for $3,409,953.21. In this sum is embraced the amount of $2,858,798.62, the judgment in the case of the Choctaw Indians, which was rendered in the Supreme Court and ordered by mandate from that court to be entered in the Court of Claims.

Two suits, claiming $662.26, were discontinued on claimants' motion.

CRIMINAL PROSECUTIONS.

There were terminated during the last year 12,905 criminal prosecutions; 227 of these were prosecutions under the customs laws, in which there were 120 convictions, 27 acquittals, and 80 were entered *nol. pros.*, discontinued, or quashed; 5,064 under the internal revenue laws, in which were 3,100 convictions, 803 acquittals, and 1,161 were entered *nol. pros.*, discontinued, or quashed; 540 under post-office laws, in which there were 302 convictions, 115 acquittals, and 123 entered *nol. pros.*, discontinued, or quashed; 96 under election laws, in which there were 45 convictions, 13 acquittals, and 38 entered *nol. pros.*, discontinued, or quashed; six under the civil rights acts, in which there were — convictions, 2 acquittals, and 4 entered *nol. pros.*, discontinued, or quashed; 298 under intercourse acts, in which there were 260 convictions, 9 acquittals, and 29 entered *nol. pros.*, discontinued, or quashed; 175 under the pension laws, in which there were 77 convictions, 27 acquittals, and 71 entered *nol. pros.*, discontinued, or quashed; 36 for embezzlement, in which there were 14 convictions, 6 acquittals, and 16 entered *nol. pros.*, discontinued, or quashed; 6,463 miscellaneous prosecutions, in which there were 4,080 convictions, 1,348 acquittals, 1,035 entered *nol. pros.*, discontinued, or quashed.

In many of the prosecutions under the internal revenue laws entered *nol. pros.*, discontinued, or quashed, a compromise and settlement were made in the internal revenue bureau of the treasury department.

Among subjects of special interest to the people of the United States we can refer with satisfaction to the action of the Department of Justice in connection with laws against Mormonism which have been on our statute books for many years and which had been practically ignored until the advent of the present administration, when, under the special direction of the President, they have been put in force with the result that offenders have been tried and punished, and that the Mormons themselves, in many instances, admit the justice of the acts of the government and govern themselves accordingly. The prosecution of timber thieves has been carried out with such vigilance that in a large measure the terrible inroads made upon the property of the nation have been put a stop to and the offenders brought to justice. In this connection we close with the views of the President relative to this department, as stated in his message to Congress indicating the improvements suggested by the attorney-general.

> The conduct of the Department of Justice for the last fiscal year is fully detailed in the report of the attorney-general, and I invite the earnest attention of the Congress to the same, and due consideration of the recommendations therein contained.
> In the report submitted by this officer to the last session of the Congress he strongly recommended the erection of a penitentiary for the confinement of prisoners convicted and sentenced in the United States courts; and he repeats the recommendation in his report for the last year.
> This is a matter of very great importance and should at once receive Congressional action. United States prisoners are now confined in more than thirty different State prisons and penitentiaries scattered in every part of the country. They are subjected to nearly as many different modes of treatment and discipline and are far too much removed from the control and regulation of the government. So far as they are entitled to humane treatment and an opportunity for improvement and reformation, the government is responsible to them and society that these things are forthcoming. But this duty can scarcely

be discharged without more absolute control and direction than is possible under the present system.

Many of our good citizens have interested themselves, with the most beneficial results, in the question of prison reform. The general government should be in a situation, since there must be United States prisoners, to furnish important aid in this movement, and should be able to illustrate what may be practically done in the direction of this reform and to present an example, in the treatment and improvement of its prisoners, worthy of imitation.

With prisons under its own control, the government could deal with the somewhat vexed question of convict labor, so far as its convicts were concerned, according to a plan of its own adoption, and with due regard to the rights and interests of our laboring citizens, instead of sometimes aiding in the operation of a system which causes among them irritation and discontent.

Upon consideration of this subject it might be thought wise to erect more than one of these institutions, located in such places as would best subserve the purposes of convenience and economy in transportation. The considerable cost of maintaining these convicts, as at present, in State institutions, would be saved by the adoption of the plan proposed; and by employing them in the manufacture of such articles as were needed for use by the government quite a large pecuniary benefit would be realized in partial return for our outlay.

I again urge a change in the federal judicial system to meet the wants of the people and obviate the delays necessarily attending the present condition of affairs in our courts. All are agreed that something should be done, and much favor is shown, by those well able to advise, to the plan suggested by the attorney-general at the last session of the Congress, and recommended in my last annual message. This recommendation is here renewed, together with another made at the same time, touching a change in the manner of compensating district attorneys and marshals; and the latter subject is commended to the Congress for its action, in the interest of economy to the government, and humanity, fairness, and justice to our people.

DEPARTMENT OF AGRICULTURE.

The President, in his message to the second session of the Forty-ninth Congress, stated that "the Department of Agriculture, representing the oldest and largest of our national industries, is subserving well the purposes of its organization. By the introduction of new subjects of farming enterprise, and by opening new sources of agricultural wealth, and the dissemination of early information concerning production and prices, it has contributed largely to the country's prosperity. Through this agency, advanced thought and investigation touching the subjects it has in charge should, among other things, be practically applied to the home production at a low cost of articles of food which are now imported from abroad. Such an innovation will necessarily, of course, in the beginning be within the domain of intelligent experiment, and the subject in every stage should receive all possible encouragement from the government." Thus indorsed by the executive, the Department of Agriculture, in charge of its experienced commissioner, Norman J. Colman, has steadily progressed under the present administration, to the great advantage of our farming population. In May, 1885, was organized the Dairy Division, for the purpose of facilitating, in every way possible, the work of this great and important industry. A complete list was obtained of all those engaged in dairying on a large scale, and then a circular was issued and widely distributed, with the view of obtaining facts and data sufficient to enable the computation to be made of the several averages of the yield per cow per day, in milk, butter, and cheese, and the average value per cow in the different States. The result of this inquiry has been to secure, for the first time, a mass of most important and reliable information relative to all matters connected with the dairy industry. This interesting report can be secured by our farmers upon writing to the Commissioner of Agriculture.

BUREAU OF ANIMAL INDUSTRY.

This highly important bureau was organized June 1, 1884, with the view of making investigations and reports upon the condition, protection, and use of the domestic animals of the United States, also as to the causes of contagious, infectious, and communicable diseases among domestic animals, and the means for the prevention and cure of the same; together with the direction and management of quarantine stations, for imported cattle. Special experienced agents are sent to all sections of the country to investigate and report upon supposed cases of pleuro-pneumonia, and a temporary quarantine of herds thus suspected is immediately ordered. The strictest scrutiny is maintained to prevent any violation of the quarantine, and to guard against the spread of pleuro-pneumonia while it is being extirpated in the quarantined district. The great importance of the work of this bureau to the interest of the farmer, and its successful results so far obtained, are universally admitted. The reports already published of the work of this bureau should be in the hands of every practical farmer, as they contain a digest of valuable information not to be found elsewhere.

DIVISION OF ENTOMOLOGY.

The work of this division covers the securing of reliable information upon all that relates to insects injurious to agriculture, and also the best means of counteracting their ravages. The entomologist, with his assistants and field agents, devotes his time to giving needed information, in the warfare which the cultivators of the soil have constantly to make against these injurious insects. The importance of this work may best be understood when we consider the vast number of insects that affect our agriculture, and the immense losses which they occasion; and in no way can this be indicated so clearly as by facts regarding losses occasioned by insects, reduced to dollars and cents.

The wheat midge in New York State, 1854, caused a loss of fifteen millions of dollars.

The damage in the Mississippi valley in 1864, done by the chinch-bug, amounted to seventy-three millions of dollars.

The Rocky Mountain locust, in 1874, damaged the crops of four States to the amount of fifty-six millions of dollars.

The cotton-worm occasioned an average annual loss, before the war, of fifteen millions of dollars.

The most careful estimates here placed the aggregate *annual* loss to American agriculture, in its broadest sense, from the injuries of insects, at from three to four millions of dollars; a sum which seems at first flash so enormous that it strikes one as inaccurate; but, notwithstanding the losses have been measurably decreased by important *remedial discoveries*, so far as the worst pests are concerned, the total loss will still remain enormous. The work of this division is best exemplified in the reports which it has made, and which are distributed gratuitously by the department. We annex titles of a few of these valuable contributions: —

Insects affecting the orange-tree.
The cotton-worm.
The mulberry silk-worm.
Insects injurious to forest-trees.
Insects affecting garden crops.
Insects affecting the hop crop.
Insects affecting the cranberry crop.

Together with many others of equal value and interest.

SECTION OF SILK CULTURE.

To those interested and who have given attention to the introduction of the growth and manufacture of silk in this country, the subject is one of absorbing interest, and it properly deserves national attention. With everything in our power, climate, manufacturing facilities, etc., there is every reason to believe that within a few years the United States will become an important factor in the growth and manufacture of silk. In this connection it is satisfactory to refer to the good work already accomplished under the above named section. An immense correspondence is carried on, and every facility afforded in the shape of practical information on the subject.

DIVISION OF CHEMISTRY.

The work of this division has proved of great practical service to the country in the analysis made of milk, Sorghum cane-juice, beet-juices, etc. The experiments in the manufacture of sugar have been very interesting, and the reports have been largely distributed for the benefit of our farming population. Space will not permit our reference to the important divisions of botany and ornithology, both of which have proved of incalculable value to the general interests of our whole country, but the total result of the good work of the Department of Agriculture will be sufficient evidence to the thinking farmer that under the present administration the interests of agriculture have not been lost sight of.

THE DEPARTMENT OF LABOR.

THE bureau of labor was established by act of Congress, approved June 27, 1884. The commissioner of labor is directed by this organic law to collect information upon the subject of labor, its relation to capital, the hours of labor, and the earnings of laboring men and women, and the means of promoting their material, social, intellectual, and moral prosperity; and annually to make a report in writing to the Secretary of the Interior of the information collected and collated by him, and containing such recommendations as he may deem calculated to promote the efficiency of the bureau.

Under the present administration the great importance of this subject of labor has received careful consideration, the result being that the bureau has been officially raised to a department the general design and duties of which shall be to acquire and diffuse among the people of the United States useful information on subjects connected with labor, in the most general and comprehensive sense of that word, and especially upon its relation to capital, the hours of labor, the earnings of laboring men and women, and the means of promoting their material, social, intellectual, and moral prosperity. The commissioner is specially charged to ascertain at as early a date as possible, and whenever industrial changes shall make it essential, the cost of producing articles at the time dutiable in the United States in leading countries where such articles are produced by fully specified units of production, and under a classification showing the different elements of cost, or approximate cost, of such articles of production, including the wages paid in such industries per day, week, month, or year, or by the piece, and hours employed per day, and the profits of the manufacturers and producers of such articles, and the comparative cost of living, and the kind of living. It shall be the duty of the commissioner, also, to ascertain and report as to the effect of the tariff, and the effect thereon of the state of the currency, in the United States, on the agricultural industry, especially as to its effect on mortgage indebtedness of farmers, and what articles are now controlled by trusts, and what effect said trusts have had on limiting production and keeping up prices.

He shall also establish a system of reports by which, at intervals of not less than two years, he can report the general condition, so far as production is concerned, of the leading industries of the country. The commissioner of labor is also specially charged to investigate the causes of and facts relating to all controversies and disputes between employers and employés as they may occur, and which may tend to interfere with the welfare of the people of the different States, and report thereon to Congress. Under the experienced and able management of Col. Carroll D. Wright the work of the bureau has been carried out in a most successful manner, the annual reports supplying the most important information from reliable data, giving the reasons for industrial depression, the "rights and wrongs of convict labor," and "strikes and lockouts between January, 1880, and December, 1886." This department has now in course of preparation reports upon "The Condition of Railroad Employés," and "The Condition of Working Women in Thirty Leading Cities in the United States." These reports have been in great demand, and have been of great service in definitely settling questions bearing upon work and wages. It would be well if every thinking laborer should secure copies for the reading of himself and friends, which will prove to him that there has been very great interest taken during the present administration in all that relates to the comfort of the workingman, and reasonable evidence given that under the same state of things there can only be progress for the better as these various statistics are collected.

THE GOVERNMENT PRINTING-OFFICE.

Although neither a department nor bureau, this office should have some notice as the one from which the enormous volume of reports, speeches, etc., finds its way all over the United States. Under the able management of Mr. Benedict the public printer, important results have been secured, which compare most favorably with the work done under previous Administrations. Some idea of this greatly increased work may be gained from the following:—

	Copies.
Copies of speeches and President's message printed on private order for Congress, from Dec. 1, 1885, to June 1, 1886, first session, Forty-ninth Congress,	2,481,880
Copies of speeches and President's message printed on private order for Congress, from Dec. 1, 1887, to June 1, 1888, first session, Fiftieth Congress. .	5,565,835
Increase	3,083,955

Statement showing the increase in bound congressional work delivered to Congress this session over that of two years ago:—

	Volumes.
Congressional work bound, complete, and delivered to Congress, from July 1, 1885, to June 1, 1886 . .	950,215
Congressional work bound, complete, and delivered to Congress, from July 1, 1887, to June 1, 1888 . .	1,312,122
Increase of volumes bound	361,907

During the year ending June 30, 1886, 6,094,785 pounds of printing and writing papers were used. This year, up to June 9, a period of eleven months and a quarter, 6,226,360 pounds of printing and writing papers were used, or an increase of sixty-five odd tons more for the eleven and a quarter months than was used in the whole twelve months of 1885–86.

The result of a recent investigation of this office indicates, that notwithstanding the enormous increase in work done, and additional cost of material, a saving of $217,000 has been effected, with 303 less employees.

THE UNITED STATES CIVIL-SERVICE COMMISSION.

To establish a reform in the working of a government, is a herculean task; and where that reform has to meet with universal prejudice, it becomes still more difficult. Reform in civil service has been the bugbear in all governments, and the barnacles of red-tape policy cling to their positions with renewed strength at every attempt at removal. In this country, on the other hand, the trouble has been that the service of the nation has suffered from the long-established custom of turning out office-holders at the beginning of a new administration. Thoughtful men, who have given their attention to the subject, saw that each year as it rolled around added a number of incompetent men to the already overloaded rolls of our various departments; and, having the good of the nation in view, an organization has been effected for the purification of public offices, and reducing the work of the Government to a business basis. The result of the influence of this third political party has been to establish the Civil-Service Commission, having for its object the proper arrangement and classification of all applications for positions; with the view that there should be no complaint as to examinations, sufficient notice is given in season for the applicants to be present at the locations selected in each State and Territory. From the fourth annual report of this commission, now passing through the press, we learn, that, during the year 1886–87, two hundred and sixty-eight examinations were held, the number of applicants examined being four thousand three hundred and twenty-seven. Of course a large proportion of these applicants were examined in Washington, to which place they would naturally come seeking office. It is a gratifying fact to know, that, according to this last report, a little more than two-thirds of those examined passed favorably, and were entered on the proper lists as available. It can be seen at once that by the addition of an experienced clerical force the general work of the Government would be more faithfully accomplished; and the result, so far as shown in the different departments, indicates better work, more rapidity in its completion, a less number of employees, and a reduction in expense. The total number of appointments in the departments under the civil-service rules, during the period covered by the report, were five hundred and forty-seven; and a visit to any of our departments, bureaus, or offices of the Government will satisfy the most incredulous of the great gain that has been derived from the working of the civil-service rules under the careful management of the commission, composed of Alfred P. Edgerton, Indiana, John H. Oberly, Illinois, and Charles Lyman, Connecticut. Under civil-service rules, each State and Territory is entitled to so many appointments, according to its population. When a clerk is needed in a department, the Civil-Service Commission is notified; and the names of the four highest in the grade desired are sent in to be selected from, these names being taken from the States whose quota has not already been filled. In this way the time and patience of heads of departments, congressmen, and others is not trenched upon; and we are saved the scandals which have existed heretofore in the greedy rush for office.

As might naturally be expected in a great work of this kind, experience would indicate improvements and changes; and, when necessary, such improvements have been made, and new rules promulgated, very much to the advantage of the service of the Government. The Civil-Service Commission make many practical suggestions for the future in their fourth annual report, which, if adopted and carried out, cannot but lead to a most valuable and perfected system in the general management of the various departments of our government. Not the least important recommendation is a new system of classification for all of the departments, by which employees are divided into ten classes, covering salaries of from $720 per annum to over $2,000. The perfect simplicity of such an arrangement must be apparent at a glance, and there is reasonable certainty that it will be adopted. The successful working of the civil-service rules in every department of our Government has been admitted to the writer by all the heads of departments and bureaus. Work is better done and more promptly, and the knowledge on the part of the employee that his or her services are permanent during good behavior is a great inducement for thorough good work. A singular and very striking evidence of this lies in the fact, that, under the present Administration, there has been an unprecedented increase in the purchase and leasing of permanent residences by clerks in the departments at Washington. No better evidence of the value of civil-service reform can be given than the following extract from the message of the President of the United States: —

"The continued operation of the law relating to our civil service has added the most convincing proofs of its necessity and usefulness. It is a fact worthy of note that every public officer who has a just idea of his duty to the people testifies to the value of this reform. Its stanchest friends are found among those who understand it best, and its warmest supporters are those who are restrained and protected by its requirements.

"The meaning of such restraint and protection is not appreciated by those who want places under the Government, regardless of merit and efficiency, nor by those who insist that the selection for such places should rest upon a proper credential showing active partisan work. They mean to public officers, if not their lives, the only opportunity afforded them to attend to public business; and they mean to the good people of the country the better performance of the work of their Government.

"It is exceedingly strange that the scope and nature of this reform are so little understood, and that so many things not included within its plan are called by its name. When cavil yields more fully to examination, the system will have large additions to the number of its friends.

"Our civil-service reform may be imperfect in some of its details; it may be misunderstood and opposed; it may not always be faithfully applied; its designs may sometimes miscarry through mistake or wilful intent; it may sometimes tremble under the assaults of its enemies, or languish under the misguided zeal of impracticable friends; but if the people of this country ever submit to the banishment of its underlying principle from the operation of their Government, they will abandon the surest guaranty of the safety and success of American institutions."

CHAPTER XIII.

ALLEN G. THURMAN.

There is one compensating feature, in our troubled and ofttimes troubling American politics, that in a measure condones for the offences of the system, and repairs the wrongs that an undue partisanship may commit. It lies in the fact that after the contentions and turmoils of party campaigns have passed, and the inflamed and exaggerated view has given place to dispassionate estimate and fair judgment, we do substantial justice to our public men, and, in the end, award to them their proper place in history. The stress of passion and of half-calumny that accompanies the discussion of public questions is an evidence of the earnestness with which our voters regard the issues before them, and the final award of praise that is given becomes all the more valuable because it is a vindication and an apology as well. To some men who are so well endowed by nature, and have so wrought during their working years that any belittling carries immediate reaction, this final justice is often done before the close of their earthly career, and sometimes even in the years of their best mental vigor and usefulness. Such has been the case of Allen G. Thurman, in whose honor all men are now pleased to speak, and who is loved and respected by many not of his political faith, and whose patriotic, honest, and honorable devotion to his country is recognized by all. That he is not in the front of public or political leadership to-day lies only in his fixed determination, made some time ago, never again to be a candidate for public place or power, but to give his final years to the quiet of that private life he always loved but of which he was for so many years deprived. We need go back no farther than the last convention of his party in this State to discover the pressure brought to bear upon him to again enter public life, nor the decided manner in which he adhered to the above described resolution.

Had affairs so shaped themselves, on several occasions when such shape seemed more than possible, as to have sent Mr. Thurman to the White House, he would have represented both the old and the new "Mother of Presidents," as Virginia gave him to the nation, and Ohio early adopted him as one of her sons. He was born in Lynchburg, Virginia, on November 13, 1813, his father being the Rev. P. Thurman, and his mother the only daughter of Colonel Nathaniel Allen, of North Carolina, nephew and adopted son of Joseph Hewes, one of the signers of the Declaration of Independence. His parents removed to Chillicothe, the old capital of Ohio, in 1819, and he made that place his home until he removed to Columbus, in 1853, where he has since resided. His education was in the Chillicothe academy, and at the hands of his mother, who was well gifted by nature and learning for that important task. He studied law under the direction of his uncle, the late William Allen, then United States senator, and afterwards Governor of Ohio; and also with Noah H. Swayne, afterwards one of the justices of the United States Supreme Court. While engaged in this duty he also gave much time to land-surveying, of which profession he was very fond, and which doubtless aided in giving him that robust strength and physical vitality that in after years enabled him to accomplish so great an amount of mental work. The preparation he had for the busy and useful life he has lived is best described by Judge Alfred Yaple, who, in a recent sketch, gives the following graphic picture:—

His mother continued to superintend his education, directing his reading of authors even after he had left the old Chillicothe academy, a private institution, and the highest and only one he ever attended until his admission to the bar. While attending this academy Thurman's classmates and intimates were sent away to college. He could not go, for not only did his parents find themselves without means to send him, but even required his exertions for their own support and the support of his sisters, a duty which he cheerfully and efficiently rendered, remaining single and at home for more than nine years after his admission to the bar, giving a large part of his earnings towards his parents' and sisters' support. The day his companions mounted the stage and went away to college he was seized with temporary despair. Sick at heart, he sought the old Presbyterian burying-ground, and lay down on a flat tomb and cried. Soon the thought struck him that it was idle and would not do. A gentleman was passing to whom he told his grief, but added, — "If they come home and have learned more than I have, they must work for it." Old citizens still remember that a light was often seen in young Thurman's room until four o'clock in the morning. He would never quit anything until he had mastered it and made it his own. This particular trait he has possessed ever since. In the acquisition of solid learning his academy fellows never got in advance of him, and he kept studying long after they had graduated. He taught school, studied and practised surveying, prepared himself for and was admitted to the bar in 1835.

Those who have watched the slow and ceaseless battle by which a young lawyer fights his way into practice and to a standing at the bar can guess the progress made by young Thurman, who in sixteen years after his admission was placed by his State upon its supreme bench. This promotion was made by no sudden leap, but came only by natural growth and after he had shown himself a master hand in his great profession. The period between the above dates was one of constant and intense mental activity. The bar of Chillicothe at that time was excelled by none in the State for ability, learning, and eloquence; but such progress did he make that in a comparatively short time he stood confessedly in the very front rank of the profession, not only in Ross County but in the State of Ohio. "Employed in almost every litigated case in Ross County," says one of his biographers, "he was retained in many important litigations in adjoining and remote counties. With this immense practice, no client could ever truthfully complain that his case was neglected. Pleadings were filed at the proper time, and, when the case was called for trial, his carefully prepared brief demonstrated that every pertinent authority had been noticed and every principle of law involved in the case thoroughly analyzed and considered. The painstaking labor which he bestowed upon the preparation of a case was remarkable."

In 1844, Mr. Thurman was nominated as the Democratic candidate of the Chillicothe district for Congress, and elected. During his service in that high position he advocated and voted for the " Wilmot proviso," and, upon the introduction of the Kansas-Nebraska bill by Mr. Douglas, he opposed the repeal of the Missouri Compromise, as an unnecessary disturbance of a fair settlement of controverted questions, the reopening of which might produce the most dire consequences. One term in Congress led him to desire to again return to the law, and he did so, declining a renomination, much to the regret of his constituents. He remained at the bar, in a great and growing practice, until 1851, when he was elected to the supreme bench of Ohio, under the new constitution, and drew the term for four years. From December, 1854, to February, 1856, he served as chief justice, and, on the expiration of his term, refused a renomination. The grand record he made, while on that bench is a part of the history of Ohio, and the wisdom he there showed gave the new court a standing and character all through the land. His opinions, contained in the first five volumes of the Ohio State reports, are notable for the clear and forcible expressions of his views and the accuracy of his statements of the law, and greatly strengthened and extended his reputation as a lawyer and jurist. On leaving the bench he returned once more to practice, the greater part of his labors being in the state and federal courts.

Judge Thurman steadily grew in mental stature, in legal reputation, and in the respect of his fellow-men, and it was easily seen that he would not be long left to the quietness he had chosen for himself. In 1867, the party to which he had always belonged, the Democratic, facing a majority of over forty-two thousand, cast against it on the previous year, looked about for a man who could give to it the splendid leadership it needed, and the prestige of a high and honored name. All eyes turned toward Judge Thurman, and at the convention of the party he was unanimously nominated to the governorship. It was a call he could not ignore, and, on accepting the leadership, he determined to make the best fight that lay within the compass of his powers and of the weapons at his command. The campaign was an intense and remarkable one, and the standard-bearer carried himself with such courage and determination that he won the respect and admiration of those who were his political foes. The question in issue was, whether the Constitution of the State should be so amended as to permit negro suffrage. The Democratic party opposed the measure. Mr. Thurman gave his personal attention to the details of the campaign, securing a perfect organization all over the State, managing all the party machinery with rare generalship and skill, and personally taking the stump, making, in the four months of the campaign, over one hundred strong

RESIDENCE OF ALLEN G. THURMAN, COLUMBUS, O.
[*From a Photograph by Urlin.*]

and masterly speeches. The result was that he defeated the amendment by over fifty thousand votes, and cut down the Republican majority of forty-two thousand, in 1866, to less than three thousand. Although a defeated candidate himself, he was the real winner of the contest, having carried for his party a majority of the General Assembly. That body, in recognition of his splendid fight, and with a view that his services should not be lost to his country, elected him to the United States Senate, as the successor of Benjamin F. Wade. He took his seat on March 4, 1869, and, from the first, assumed a leading commanding position in that notable body. He was no new and untried man, but one of national reputation, and known everywhere as the possessor of great power as a debater and lawyer, and a master of the diplomacy of politics. From the day of his entrance to the Senate, he was recognized as the leader of the Democratic minority, and for twelve years held that post of responsibility without question and without a rival. He was made a member of the committee on judiciary, and, on the accession of his party to power, in the Senate of the Forty-sixth Congress, he was made chairman of that important committee, and also elected to the position of president *pro tempore*, and, because of illness of Vice-President Wheeler, was compelled to preside a fair portion of the time.

Ohio was carried by the Republicans in 1872, by a majority of nearly forty thousand, and the chances of their opponents, in the year following, looked meagre and discouraging. Senator Thurman studied the situation carefully, and decided there was a chance for his party, and, under his direction, and the spur of his enthusiasm, the State was organized, a hard fight made, and won. Both branches of the Legislature were carried, and the victory was signalized by a return of Mr. Thurman to the Senate, for another term of six years. His power and influence there were recognized and acknowledged by those who were not of his political faith, as well as those who were. He was looked upon as one of the wise and great statesmen of the day, and, no matter how much one might condemn his political belief, there was no one who doubted his personal honor or his earnest and high-minded patriotism. His services to the public were invaluable. A recent biography of Senator Thurman, in referring to this phase of his public life, says : —

Perhaps he is entitled to be most commended and longest remembered for introducing, advocating with consummate skill and ability, and causing to be passed, an act since known as the " Thurman Act," relating to the Pacific railroads. By this act, it is said that more than one hundred million dollars were saved to the people as an immediate or prospective result. The opposition to the passage of this act was unscrupulous, the friends of the railroads employing every means, influence, and argument, both in and out of the Senate, to defeat it. The bill, as was asserted, with great vehemence, was unconstitutional, but its constitutionality was clearly established by Mr. Thurman, in a speech of great power, and his position in this respect has since been sustained by a decision of the Supreme

Court of the United States. Senator Thurman was not led to introduce and advocate the passage of this measure because of any fanatical opposition to railroad corporations, as such, but simply to establish and secure what he believed to be the plain contract rights of the government.

Space will allow no extended mention of his services while in the Senate. They are a part of our country, and stand on a permanent record. So valuable were they, and in such manner had he carried himself, that suggestions came from all parts of the country, that the National Democratic Convention of 1876 should honor him in nomination for the Presidency. The result was that his friends saw for him as good a chance in St. Louis as lay before any man, and that chance would, undoubtedly, have materialized into fact had not a division arisen in the Ohio delegation, and opposing ambitions kept him from having the undivided support of his State. The cold, simple fact of history is, whether pleasant to all or not, that the friends of other candidates prevailed on William Allen to stand forth as an aspirant, when they knew he could not be nominated, and in expectation that Ohio would thus be kept powerless for Thurman, through a divided delegation. The scheme worked, and the Ohio senator was not presented to the convention, and the nomination went to New York. In 1880 there was even a more determined and outspoken expression in his favor. The Democratic State Convention unanimously adopted resolutions in his favor, and instructed the delegation from Ohio to vote for him, and support him in the national convention. The first ballot in the last named body gave Senator Thurman the entire vote of the Ohio delegation, with considerable support from other States. He also received the vote of Ohio on the second ballot, and some from other States; "but, before the conclusion of that ballot, it became manifest that General Hancock would be nominated, and the vote of all the States was changed to the latter, with the single exception of Indiana, which State adhered to ex-Senator Hendricks to the last." A close observer of the times, and one who knew much of Senator Thurman and the incidents surrounding that convention, has said : —

Senator Thurman has been almost universally acknowledged by the Democracy of the country as the ablest and best representative of the party, and, from his long and eminent services rendered to the party and country, the most entitled to be honored by it. Motives of policy undoubtedly prevented the convention from nominating Thurman, not because he was not popular, for no man before the convention has as many friends or fewer enemies, but he lived in Ohio, a State, under all ordinary circumstances, certainly Republican. And, as the October election in that State for State officers would be regarded as a test of the strength of the presidential candidate in November, it was feared that the Democracy, with all of Senator Thurman's popularity in the State, would not be able to wrest it from the Republicans, with a favorite son, in the person of General Garfield, as their candidate. The apprehension that the moral effect of the defeat of the Democracy in Ohio, in October, might be disastrous to success, with Thurman as the candidate, was probably unduly magnified by the immediate friends of other candidates.

When Mr. Thurman retired from the Senate, on March 4, 1881, he did so with the expectation of laying down all public burdens, and giving himself to the pleasant quiet of private life, where he could enjoy the society of his family and his books. But the powers that be willed otherwise, and the admiration and friendship that President Garfield had always held for his Ohio neighbor were shown by an appointment of the latter as one of the representatives of the American government in the international congress to be held in Paris in 1881, where an attempt would be made to agree if possible on the fixing of a uniform rule by which silver should be regarded as money by the countries therein represented. He accepted the position because of the pleasant manner in which it would allow him to make a trip to Europe, a thing he had always desired but had never had leisure to accomplish. He sailed from New York on April 5, 1881, and returned in the following October, having meanwhile visited Switzerland, Belgium, England, and Scotland. Soon after his return he was chosen as one of the advisory commission in the troubles as to differential rates between trunk-line railroads leading from the Atlantic seaboard to the West. In this capacity he was of great service, as his wide acquaintance with all public questions, his knowledge of the country, his studies in connection with railroad problems while in the Senate, and the natural logic and fairness of his mind aided him to a comprehensive view and just conclusions.

His determination to remain in private life was once more thwarted in 1884, when the Democratic State Convention of Ohio, against his purpose and protest, sent him as a delegate at large to the national Democratic convention in Chicago, where he did good and patriotic service for his party. He was again and again mentioned while there in connection with the presidential nomination, but would not allow himself to be spoken of, or even considered as a candidate. In the State convention of the year 1885, a most determined effort was made to persuade him to accept the nomination for Governor, but he firmly and emphatically declined.

Such success and fame as Allen G. Thurman has won came not from any sudden freak of fortune, but grew as the legitimate superstructure of the foundations he had carefully laid. His life is a text-book of instruction to the young men of America. I have not done it full justice in the above, as the incidents and illustrations that give grace and flavor to a man's record, and that bring the reader into sympathy with him, were perforce omitted, and only the bare outline laid down. But enough has been said to show that industry, honesty, and a concession to the rights of others have ever been among the strong points of his character. In the early days, when building up a practice at the bar, he made a point to attend to the interests of his clients with the most exact care and faithfulness. His pleadings were filed at the proper time, and when the case was called he was always ready, with a carefully prepared brief that showed that every pertinent authority had been noticed and every principle of law involved in the case thoroughly analyzed and considered. No labor was too great, and no detail so small that it was not weighed and given its due attention. He was able and adroit in the trial of a case, and the weak point of an adversary was always discovered and attacked. His ability to class and generalize was always great, and his logic of the solid and convincing order. He has always been a Democrat as a matter of conviction, and his belief in the principles of his party has been such that he has sometimes manfully stood by it when all its declarations did not conform to his judgment, in the hope and expectation that it would surely return to all the tenets of the ancient faith. As a public speaker he is forcible and direct, wasting no time on trivial points, and so carrying and expressing himself as to compel the hearer to concede that he is uttering the faith that is within him. While in the Senate he always received marked attention from the public, and an announcement that he was to speak would always secure a large attendance of spectators and fellow-senators.

While in that body he was never a mere partisan, and he always held the respect of his political opponents.

The gravity, strength, and high mental stature of Senator Thurman were so well recognized after his first few years in the Senate that the title of the " Old Roman " was soon attached to him, and has since remained, as Jackson became " Old Hickory,"

Benton "Old Bullion," and Douglas the "Little Giant." The appellation has a sturdy suggestion, that is readily adopted by those who know the plain and simple manner in which he carries his honors, and the aversion he holds towards all forms of cant, hypocrisy, or ornamental display. As one has said of him, —

He is a perfect type of the straightforward, strong-hearted, clear-headed, Westerner. He is plain in dress and manner, and, barring the red bandanna handkerchief, which has become a part of American history, there is nothing about him to break the monotony of the darkish, loose-fitting suit in which he is always attired..

From this it must not for a moment be imagined that he lacks culture, or has lost anything of the grace of the old school of manners, that was constantly before him in the early days of his career. He is one of the most thoroughly learned men in public life in the country. He is a fine French scholar, and among his favorite books are the works of the early French dramatists, which he reads in the original. He has a large and well selected library, that touches in some form on every point of the world's literature. He has a genius for mathematics, and is frequently occupied in working out abstruse and intricate problems. He is resolute, serious, and emphatic in all the tasks he has in hand, and, when they are accomplished, enjoys a quiet sociability, his talk pleasant and humorous, and full of illustrative anecdotes. His days in these latter years of quiet are mostly spent at his pleasant home in Columbus. He has enough of this world's goods to keep him comfortably the rest of his life, although his fortune is small; every dollar of it is his own earnings, and no shadow of suspicion ever fell into the minds of any as to his methods of obtaining it. One of his most pleasant memories, as he reviews the long and busy life he has lived, must lie in the fact that, even in the wildest ventures of party detraction and the most frenzied forms of political warfare, no hint has ever been heard against his personal honor, or his honesty as a man or public official. Surrounded by the good-will and good-wishes of his home community, honored by the American people everywhere as a great and patriotic man, secure in the fame he has so ably earned, and allowed to see that he is strong in the affections and respect of many who have in the past bitterly opposed him in public and political life, his lot is indeed a favored one, and his sun is going down in peace.

We have selected the above admirable sketch of Senator Thurman, as prepared by H. J. Seymour and published in the Magazine of Western History, 1885, as the best and most complete epitome of his life. The fact of his unanimous nomination for Vice-President of the United States, at the St. Louis convention, is conclusive evidence of the correctness and justice of the preceding remarks. Mr. Thurman's letter of acceptance, which will be found in our concluding chapter, breathes that fair, honest spirit of national independence which is bound to win.

The members of the Democratic Notification

Committee called on Judge Thurman, June 28, at his residence, Columbus, Ohio. General Collins spoke as follows: —

JUDGE THURMAN, — We bear a message from the great council of your party. It is but a formal notice of your nomination by that body for the high office of Vice-President of the United States. Rich as our language is in power and expression, it contains no words to adequately convey the sentiment of that convention as its heart went out to you. I present my friend, the Hon. Charles D. Jacob, Mayor of Louisville.

Mr. Jacob stepped forward, and, in an earnest voice, read the following formal letter of notification: —

COLUMBUS, Ohio, June 28, 1888.

To the Hon. Allen G. Thurman of Ohio, —

SIR, — It has become the highly agreeable duty of this committee to inform you that upon the first ballot of the National Democratic Convention, held recently in the city of St. Louis, and representing every State and Territory of our Union, for the purpose of selecting candidates for the Presidency and Vice-Presidency, you were unanimously chosen as the nominee of that great party, for the eminent and responsible office of Vice-President of the United States. In thus spontaneously and emphatically demanding a return to that political arena which you graced with so much wisdom, dignity, and vigor, the Democracy of this country have honored themselves by relieving their party from the charge of ingratitude, and we believe and trust, in November next, the people will efface such a taint from the republic by electing you to preside over the most august deliberative body in the world — the Senate of the United States. [Applause.] Should so desirable a consummation be achieved, then, indeed, could every lover of his country, regardless of party or creed, rejoice that in you is embraced the highest type of the enlightened and refined American citizen, and that, no matter what the crisis might be, this government would be safe in your hands. [Applause.]

An engrossed copy of the platform of principles, couched in language that admits of no doubt, and adopted without a dissenting vote, is herewith presented.

In discharging their trust this committee desire to convey to you assurances of the most profound esteem and admiration, and to express their sincerest good-wishes for your happiness and prosperity. We have the honor, sir, to be your obedient servants.

        PATRICK COLLINS, Chairman, Massachusetts.
        BASIL GORDON, Secretary, Virginia.

Amid the profound silence, Judge Thurman replied as follows: —

MR. CHAIRMAN AND GENTLEMEN OF THE COMMITTEE, — I pray you to accept my very sincere thanks for the kind and courteous manner in which you have communicated to me the official information of my nomination by the St. Louis convention. You know without saying it that I am profoundly grateful to the convention and to the Democratic party for the honor conferred upon me, and the more so that it was wholly unsought and undesired by me; not that I undervalued a distinction which any man of our party, however eminent, might highly prize, but simply because I had ceased to be ambitious of public life. But when I am told in so earnest and impressive a manner that I can still render service to the good cause to which I have ever been devoted — a cause to which I am bound by the ties of affection, by the dictates of judgment, by a sense of obligation for favors so often conferred upon me, and by a fervent hope that the party may long continue to be able to serve the republic, what can I under such circumstances do but yield my private wishes to the demand of those whose opinions I am bound to respect? [Applause.] Gentlemen, with an unfeigned diffidence in my ability to fulfil the expectations that led to my nomination, I yet feel it to be my duty to accept it, and do all that it may be in my power to do to merit so marked a distinction.

Gentlemen, the country is blessed by an able and honest administration of the general government. [Applause.] We have a President who wisely, bravely, diligently, and patriotically discharges the duties of his high office. [Applause.] I fully believe that the best interests of the country require his reëlection, and the hope that I may be able to contribute somewhat to bring about the result is one of my motives for accepting a place on our ticket, and I also feel it my duty to labor for a reduction of taxes, and to put a stop to that accumulation of a surplus in the treasury that, in my judgment, is not only prejudicial to our financial welfare, but is in a high degree dangerous to honest and constitutional government. [Applause.] I suppose, gentlemen, that I need say no more to-day. In due time, and in accordance with established usage, I will transmit to your chairman a written acceptance of my nomination, with such observations upon public questions as may seem to me to be proper. [Applause.]

THE CAPITOL, WASHINGTON, D.C.

CHAPTER XIII.

CAMPAIGN OF 1888. — OFFICIAL DOCUMENTS.

TARIFF MESSAGE. — DEMOCRATIC PLATFORM. — CIVIL SERVICE MESSAGE.

In this, the concluding chapter of our work, it is our province to show that the programme of the Democratic party is to continue the good work so well commenced, and to that end we invite the attention of our readers to the documents which follow, feeling convinced that a careful perusal of the same will secure conviction to the minds of all: —

TARIFF MESSAGE

OF THE PRESIDENT OF THE UNITED STATES, COMMUNICATED TO THE TWO HOUSES OF CONGRESS AT THE BEGINNING OF THE FIRST SESSION OF THE FIFTIETH CONGRESS.

To the Congress of the United States, — You are confronted at the threshold of your legislative duties with a condition of the national finances which imperatively demands immediate and careful consideration.

The amount of money annually exacted, through the operation of present laws, from the industries and necessities of the people, largely exceeds the sum necessary to meet the expenses of the government.

When we consider that the theory of our institutions guarantees to every citizen the full enjoyment of all the fruits of his industry and enterprise, with only such deduction as may be his share towards the careful and economical maintenance of the government which protects him, it is plain that the exaction of more than this is indefensible extortion, and a culpable betrayal of American fairness and justice. This wrong inflicted upon those who bear the burden of national taxation, like other wrongs, multiplies a brood of evil consequences. The public treasury, which should only exist as a conduit conveying the people's tribute to its legitimate objects of expenditure, becomes a hoarding-place for money needlessly withdrawn from trade and the people's use, thus crippling our national energies, suspending our country's development, preventing investment in productive enterprise, threatening financial disturbance, and inviting schemes of public plunder.

This condition of our treasury is not altogether new; and it has more than once of late been submitted to the people's representatives in the Congress, who alone can apply a remedy. And yet the situation still continues, with aggravated incidents, more than ever presaging financial convulsion and widespread disaster.

It will not do to neglect this situation because its dangers are not now palpably imminent and apparent. They exist none the less certainly, and await the unforeseen and unexpected occasion when suddenly they will be precipitated upon us.

On the thirtieth day of June, 1885, the excess of revenues over public expenditures, after complying with the annual requirement of the sinking-fund act, was $17,859,735.84; during the year ended June 30, 1886, such excess amounted to $49,405,545.20; and during the year ended June 30, 1887, it reached the sum of $55,567,849.54.

The annual contributions to the sinking fund during the three years above specified, amounting in the aggregate to $138,058,320.94, and deducted from the surplus as stated, were made by calling in for that purpose outstanding three per cent. bonds of the government. During the six months prior to June 30, 1887, the surplus revenue had grown so large by repeated accumulations, and it was feared the withdrawal of this great sum of money needed by the people would so affect the business of the country, that the sum of $79,864,100 of such surplus was applied to the payment of the principal and interest of the three per cent. bonds still outstanding, and which were then payable at the option of the government. The precarious condition of financial affairs among the people still needing relief, immediately after the thirtieth day of June, 1887, the remainder of the three per cent. bonds then outstanding, amounting with principal and interest to the sum of $18,877,500, were called in and applied to the sinking-fund contribution for the current fiscal year. Notwithstanding these operations of the Treasury Department, representations of distress in business circles not only continued but increased, and absolute peril seemed at hand. In these circumstances, the contribution to the sinking fund for the current fiscal year was at once completed by the expenditure of $27,684,283.55 in the purchase of government bonds not yet due bearing four and four and a half per cent. interest, the premium paid thereon averaging about twenty-four per cent. for the former and eight per cent. for the latter. In addition to this, the interest accruing during the current year upon the outstanding bonded indebtedness of the government was to some extent anticipated, and banks selected as depositories of public money were permitted to somewhat increase their deposits.

While the expedients thus employed to release to the people the money lying idle in the Treasury served to avert immediate danger, our surplus revenues have continued to accumulate, the excess for the present year amounting on the first day of December to $55,258,701.19, and estimated to reach the sum of $113,000,000 on the 30th of June next, at which date it is expected that this sum, added to prior accumulations, will swell the surplus in the treasury to $140,000,000.

There seems to be no assurance that, with such a withdrawal from use of the people's circulating medium, our business community may not in the near future be subjected to the same distress which was quite lately produced from the same cause. And while the functions of our National Treasury should be few and simple, and while its best condition would be reached, I believe, by its entire disconnection with private business interests, yet when, by a perversion of its purposes, it idly holds money uselessly subtracted from the channels of trade, there seems to be reason for the claim that some legitimate means should be devised by the government to restore in an emergency, without waste or extravagance, such money to its place among the people.

If such an emergency arises, there now exists no clear and

undoubted executive power of relief. Heretofore the redemption of three per cent. bonds, which were payable at the option of the government, has afforded a means for the disbursement of the excess of our revenues; but these bonds have all been retired, and there are no bonds outstanding the payment of which we have the right to insist upon. The contribution to the sinking fund which furnishes the occasion for expenditure in the purchase of bonds has been already made for the current year, so that there is no outlet in that direction.

In the present state of legislation, the only pretence of any existing executive power to restore, at this time, any part of our surplus revenues to the people by its expenditure, consists in the supposition that the Secretary of the Treasury may enter the market and purchase the bonds of the government not yet due, at a rate of premium to be agreed upon. The only provision of law from which such a power could be derived is found in an appropriation bill passed a number of years ago; and it is subject to the suspicion that it was intended as temporary and limited in its application, instead of conferring a continuing discretion and authority. No condition ought to exist which would justify the grant of power to a single official, upon his judgment of its necessity, to withhold from or release to the business of the people, in an unusual manner, money held in the Treasury, and thus affect, at his will, the financial situation of the country; and if it is deemed wise to lodge in the Secretary of the Treasury the authority in the present juncture to purchase bonds, it should be plainly vested, and provided, as far as possible, with such checks and limitations as will define this official's right and discretion, and at the same time relieve him from undue responsibility.

In considering the question of purchasing bonds as a means of restoring to circulation the surplus money accumulating in the treasury, it should be borne in mind that premiums must of course be paid upon such purchase, that there may be a large part of these bonds held as investments which cannot be purchased at any price, and that combinations among holders who are willing to sell may unreasonably enhance the cost of such bonds to the government.

It has been suggested that the present bonded debt might be refunded at a less rate of interest, and the difference between the old and new security paid in cash, thus finding use for the surplus in the treasury. The success of this plan, it is apparent, must depend upon the volition of the holders of the present bonds; and it is not entirely certain that the inducement which must be offered them would result in more financial benefit to the government than the purchase of bonds, while the latter proposition would reduce the principal of the debt by actual payment, instead of extending it.

The proposition to deposit the money held by the government in banks throughout the country, for use by the people, is, it seems to me, exceedingly objectionable in principle, as establishing too close a relationship between the operations of the government treasury and the business of the country, and too extensive a commingling of their money, thus fostering an unnatural reliance in private business upon public funds. If this scheme should be adopted, it should only be done as a temporary expedient to meet an urgent necessity. Legislative and executive effort should generally be in the opposite direction, and should have a tendency to divorce, as much and as fast as can safely be done, the treasury department from private enterprise.

Of course it is not expected that unnecessary and extravagant appropriations will be made for the purpose of avoiding the accumulation of an excess of revenue. Such expenditure, beside the demoralization of all just conceptions of public duty which it entails, stimulates a habit of reckless improvidence not in the least consistent with the mission of our people or the high and beneficent purposes of our government.

I have deemed it my duty to thus bring to the knowledge of my countrymen, as well as to the attention of their representatives charged with the responsibility of legislative relief, the gravity of our financial situation. The failure of the Congress heretofore to provide against the dangers which it was quite evident the very nature of the difficulty must necessarily produce caused a condition of financial distress and apprehension since your last adjournment, which taxed to the utmost all the authority and expedients within executive control; and these appear now to be exhausted. If disaster results from the continued inaction of Congress, the responsibility must rest where it belongs.

Though the situation thus far considered is fraught with danger which should be fully realized, and though it presents features of wrong to the people as well as peril to the country, it is but a result growing out of a perfectly palpable and apparent cause, constantly reproducing the same alarming circumstances — a congested national treasury and a depleted monetary condition in the business of the country. It need hardly be stated that, while the present situation demands a remedy, we can only be saved from a like predicament in the future by the removal of its cause.

Our scheme of taxation, by means of which this needless surplus is taken from the people and put into the public treasury, consists of a tariff or duty levied upon importations from abroad, and internal revenue taxes levied upon the consumption of tobacco and spirituous and malt liquors. It must be conceded that none of the things subjected to internal-revenue taxation are, strictly speaking, necessaries; there appears to be no just complaint of this taxation by the consumers of these articles, and there seems to be nothing so well able to bear the burden without hardship to any portion of the people.

But our present tariff laws, the vicious, inequitable, and illogical source of unnecessary taxation, ought to be at once revised and amended. These laws, as their primary and plain effect, raise the price to consumers of all articles imported and subject to duty by precisely the sum paid for such duties. Thus the amount of the duty measures the tax paid by those who purchase for use these imported articles. Many of these things, however, are raised or manufactured in our own country, and the duties now levied upon foreign goods and products are called protection to these home manufactures, because they render it possible for those of our people who are manufacturers to make these taxed articles and sell them for a price equal to that demanded for the imported goods that have paid customs duty. So it happens that, while comparatively a few use the imported articles, millions of our people, who never used and never saw any of the foreign products, purchase and use things of the same kind made in this country, and pay therefor nearly or quite the same enhanced price which the duty adds to the imported articles. Those who buy imports pay the duty charged thereon into the public treasury, but the great majority of our citizens, who buy domestic articles of the same class, pay a sum at least approximately equal to this duty to the home manufacturer. This reference to the operation of our tariff laws is not made by way of instruction, but in order that we may be constantly reminded of the manner in which they impose a burden upon those who consume domestic products as well as those who consume imported articles, and thus create a tax upon all our people.

It is not proposed to entirely relieve the country of this taxation. It must be extensively continued as the source of the government's income; and in a readjustment of our tariff the interests of American labor engaged in manufacture should be carefully considered, as well as the preservation of our manufacturers. It may be called protection, or by any other name, but relief from the hardships and dangers of our present tariff laws should be devised with especial precaution against imperilling the existence of our manufacturing interests. But this existence should not mean a condition which, without regard to the public welfare or a national exigency, must always insure the realization of immense profits instead of moderately profitable returns. As the volume and diversity of our national activities increase, new recruits are added to those who desire a continuation of the advantages which they conceive the present system of tariff taxation directly affords them. So stubbornly have all efforts to reform the present condition been resisted by those of our fellow-citizens thus engaged that they can hardly complain of the suspicion, entertained to a certain extent, that there exists an organized combination all along the line to maintain their advantage.

We are in the midst of centennial celebrations, and with becoming pride we rejoice in American skill and ingenuity, in American energy and enterprise, and in the wonderful natural advantages and resources developed by a century's national growth. Yet when an attempt is made to justify a scheme which permits a tax to be laid upon every consumer in the land for the benefit of our manufacturers, quite beyond a reasonable demand for governmental regard, it suits the purposes of advocacy to call our manufactures infant industries, still needing the highest and greatest degree of favor and fostering care that can be wrung from federal legislation.

It is also said that the increase in the price of domestic manufactures resulting from the present tariff is necessary in order that higher wages may be paid to our workingmen employed in manufactories than are paid for what is called the pauper labor of Europe. All will acknowledge the force of an argument which involves the welfare and liberal compensation of our laboring people. Our labor is honorable in the eyes of every American citizen; and, as it lies at the foundation of our development and progress, it is entitled, without affectation or hypocrisy, to the utmost regard. The standard of our laborers' life should not be measured by that of any other country less favored, and they are entitled to their full share of all our advantages.

By the last census it is made to appear that, of the 17,392,099 of our population engaged in all kinds of industries, 7,670,493 are employed in agriculture, 4,074,238 in professional and personal service (2,934,876 of whom are domestic servants and laborers), while 1,810,256 are employed in trade and transportation, and 3,837,112 are classed as employed in manufacturing and mining.

For present purposes, however, the last number given should be considerably reduced. Without attempting to enumerate all, it will be conceded that there should be deducted from those which it includes 375,143 carpenters and joiners, 285,401 milliners, dressmakers, and seamstresses, 172,726 blacksmiths, 133,756 tailors and tailoresses, 102,473 masons, 76,241 butchers, 41,309 bakers, 22,083 plasterers, and 4,891 engaged in manufacturing agricultural implements, amounting in the aggregate to 1,214,023, leaving 2,623,089 persons employed in such manufacturing industries as are claimed to be benefited by a high tariff.

To these the appeal is made to save their employment and maintain their wages by resisting a change. There should be no disposition to answer such suggestions by the allegation that they are in a minority among those who labor, and therefore should forego an advantage, in the interest of low prices for the majority; their compensation, as it may be affected by the operation of tariff laws, should at all times be scrupulously kept in view; and yet, with slight reflection, they will not overlook the fact that they are consumers with the rest; that they, too, have their own wants and those of their families to supply from their earnings, and that the price of the necessaries of life, as well as the amount of their wages, will regulate the measure of their welfare and comfort.

But the reduction of taxation demanded should be so measured as not to necessitate or justify either the loss of employment by the workingman, nor the lessening of his wages; and the profits still remaining to the manufacturer, after a necessary readjustment, should furnish no excuse for the sacrifice of the interests of his employés, either in their opportunity to work or in the diminution of their compensation. Nor can the worker in manufactures fail to understand that, while a high tariff is claimed to be necessary to allow the payment of remunerative wages, it certainly results in a very large increase in the price of nearly all sorts of manufactures, which, in almost countless forms, he needs for the use of himself and his family. He receives at the desk of his employer his wages, and perhaps before he reaches his home is obliged, in a purchase for family use of an article which embraces his own labor, to return in the payment of the increase in price which the tariff permits the hard-earned compensation of many days of toil.

The farmer and the agriculturist, who manufactures nothing, but who pays the increased price which the tariff imposes, upon every agricultural implement, upon all he wears and upon all he uses and owns, except the increase of his flocks and herds, and such things as his husbandry produces from the soil, is invited to aid in maintaining the present situation, and he is told that a high duty on imported wool is necessary for the benefit of those who have sheep to shear, in order that the price of their wool may be increased. They, of course, are not reminded that the farmer who has no sheep is by this scheme obliged, in his purchases of clothing and woollen goods, to pay a tribute to his fellow-farmer as well as to the manufacturer and merchant; nor is any mention made of the fact that the sheep-owners themselves and their households must wear clothing, and use other articles manufactured from the wool they sell at tariff prices, and thus as consumers must return their share of this increased price to the tradesman.

I think it may be fairly assumed that a large proportion of the sheep owned by the farmers throughout the country are found in small flocks, numbering from twenty-five to fifty. The duty on the grade of imported wool which these sheep yield is 10 cents each pound if of the value of 30 cents or less, and 12 cents if of the value of more than 30 cents. If the liberal estimate of six pounds be allowed for each fleece, the duty thereon would be 60 or 72 cents, and this may be taken as the utmost enhancement of its price to the farmer by reason of this duty. Eighteen dollars would thus represent the increased price of the wool from twenty-five sheep, and $36 that from the wool of fifty sheep; and at present values this addition would amount to about one-third of its price. If upon its sale the farmer receives this or a less tariff profit, the wool leaves his hands charged with precisely that sum, which in all its changes will adhere to it, until it reaches the consumer. When manufactured into cloth and other goods and material for use, its cost is not only increased to the extent of the farmer's tariff profit, but a further sum has been added for the benefit of the manufacturer under the operation of other tariff laws. In the meantime, the day arrives when the farmer finds it necessary to purchase woollen goods and material to clothe himself and family for the winter. When he faces the tradesman for that purpose, he discovers that he is obliged not only to return in the way of increased prices his tariff profit on the wool he sold, and which then perhaps lies before him in manufactured form, but that he must add a considerable sum thereto to meet a further increase in cost caused by a tariff duty on the manufacture. Thus in the end he is aroused to the fact that he has paid upon a moderate purchase, as a result of the tariff scheme, which, when he sold his wool, seemed so profitable, an increase in price more than sufficient to sweep away all the tariff profit he received upon the wool he produced and sold.

When the number of farmers engaged in wool-raising is compared with all the farmers in the country, and the small proportion they bear to our population is considered; when it is made apparent that, in the case of a large part of those who own sheep, the benefit of the present tariff on wool is illusory; and, above all, when it must be conceded that the increase of the cost of living caused by such tariff becomes a burden upon those with moderate means and the poor, the employed and unemployed, the sick and well, and the young and old, and that it constitutes a tax which, with relentless grasp, is fastened upon the clothing of every man, woman, and child in the land, reasons are suggested why the removal or reduction of this duty should be included in a revision of our tariff laws.

In speaking of the increased cost to the consumer of our home manufactures, resulting from a duty laid upon imported articles of the same description, the fact is not overlooked that competition among our domestic producers sometimes has the effect of keeping the price of their products below the highest limit allowed by such duty. But it is notorious that this competition is too often strangled by combinations quite prevalent at this time, and frequently called trusts, which have for their object the regulation of the supply and price of commodities made and sold by members of the combination. The people can hardly hope for any consideration in the operation of these selfish schemes.

If, however, in the absence of such combination, a healthy and free competition reduces the price of any particular dutiable article of home production, below the limit which it might otherwise reach under our tariff laws, and if, with such reduced price, its manufacture continues to thrive, it is entirely evident that one thing has been discovered which should be carefully scrutinized in an effort to reduce taxation.

The necessity of combination to maintain the price of any commodity to the tariff point furnishes proof that some one is willing to accept lower prices for such commodity, and that such prices are remunerative; and lower prices produced by competition prove the same thing. Thus where either of these conditions exists a case would seem to be presented for an easy reduction of taxation.

The considerations which have been presented touching our tariff laws are intended only to enforce an earnest recommendation that the surplus revenues of the government be prevented by the reduction of our customs duties, and, at the same time, to emphasize a suggestion that in accomplishing this purpose we may discharge a double duty to our people by granting to them a measure of relief from tariff taxation in quarters where it is most needed and from sources where it can be most fairly and justly accorded.

Nor can the presentation made of such considerations be, with any degree of fairness, regarded as evidence of unfriendliness toward our manufacturing interests, or of any lack of appreciation of their value and importance.

These interests constitute a leading and most substantial element of our national greatness and furnish the proud proof of our country's progress. But if in the emergency that presses upon us our manufacturers are asked to surrender something for the public good and to avert disaster, their patriotism, as well as a grateful recognition of advantages already afforded, should lead them to willing coöperation. No demand is made that they shall forego all the benefits of governmental regard; but they cannot fail to be admonished of their duty, as well as their enlightened self-interest and safety, when they are reminded of the fact that financial panic and collapse, to which the present condition tends, afford no greater shelter or protection to our manufactures than to our other important enterprises. Opportunity for safe, careful, and deliberate reform is now offered; and none of us should be unmindful of a time when an abused and irritated people, heedless of those who have resisted timely and reasonable relief, may insist upon a radical and sweeping rectification of their wrongs.

The difficulty attending a wise and fair revision of our tariff laws is not underestimated. It will require on the part of the Congress great labor and care, and especially a broad and national contemplation of the subject, and a patriotic disregard of such local and selfish claims as are unreasonable and reckless of the welfare of the entire country.

Under our present laws more than four thousand articles are subject to duty. Many of these do not in any way compete with our own manufactures, and many are hardly worth attention as subjects of revenue. A considerable reduction can be made in the aggregate by adding them to the free list. The taxation of luxuries presents no features of hardship; but the necessaries of life used and consumed by all the people, the duty upon which adds to the cost of living in every home, should be greatly cheapened.

The radical reduction of the duties imposed on raw material used in manufactures, or its free importation, is of course an important factor in any effort to reduce the price of these necessaries; it would not only relieve them from the increased cost caused by the tariff on such material, but, the manufactured product being thus cheapened, that part of the tariff now laid upon such product, as a compensation to our manufacturers for the present price of raw material, could be accordingly modified. Such reduction, or free importation, would serve beside to largely reduce the revenue. It is not apparent how such a change can have any injurious effect upon our manufacturers. On the contrary, it would appear to give them a better chance in foreign markets with the manufacturers of other countries, who cheapen their wares by free material. Thus our people might have the opportunity of extending their sales beyond the limits of home consumption — saving them from the depression, interruption in business, and loss caused by a glutted domestic market, and affording their employés more certain and steady labor, with its resulting quiet and contentment.

The question thus imperatively presented for solution should be approached in a spirit higher than partisanship and considered in the light of that regard for patriotic duty which should characterize the action of those intrusted with the weal of a confiding people. But the obligation to declared party policy and principle is not wanting to urge prompt and effective action. Both of the great political parties now represented in the government have, by repeated and authoritative declarations, condemned the condition of our laws which permit the collection from the people of unnecessary revenue, and have, in the most solemn manner, promised its correction; and neither as citizens nor partisans are our countrymen in a mood to condone the deliberate violation of these pledges.

Our progress toward a wise conclusion will not be improved by dwelling upon the theories of protection and free trade. This savors too much of bandying epithets. It is a *condition* which confronts us — not a theory. Relief from this condition may involve a slight reduction of the advantages which we award our home productions, but the entire withdrawal of such advantages should not be contemplated. The question of free trade is absolutely irrelevant; and the persistent claim made in certain quarters, that all efforts to relieve the people from unjust and unnecessary taxation are schemes of so-called free-traders, is mischievous and far removed from any consideration for the public good.

The simple and plain duty which we owe the people is to reduce taxation to the necessary expenses of an economical operation of the government, and to restore to the business of the country the money which we hold in the treasury through the perversion of governmental powers. These things can and should be done with safety to all our industries, without danger to the opportunity for remunerative labor which our workingmen need, and with benefit to them and all our people, by cheapening their means of subsistence and increasing the measure of their comforts.

The Constitution provides that the President "shall, from time to time, give to the Congress information of the state of the Union." It has been the custom of the executive, in compliance with this provision, to annually exhibit to the Congress, at the opening of its session, the general condition of the country, and to detail with some particularity the operations of the different executive departments. It would be especially agreeable to follow this course at the present time, and to call attention to the valuable accomplishments of these departments during the last fiscal year. But I am so much impressed with the paramount importance of the subject to which this communication has thus far been devoted that I shall forego the addition of any other topic, and only urge upon your immediate consideration the "state of the Union" as shown in the present consideration of our treasury and our general fiscal situation, upon which every element of our safety and prosperity depends.

The reports of the heads of departments, which will be submitted, contain full and explicit information touching the transaction of the business intrusted to them, and such recommendations relating to legislation in the public interests as they deem advisable. I ask for these reports and recommendations the deliberate examination and action of the legislative branch of the government.

There are other subjects, not embraced in the departmental reports, demanding legislative consideration, and which I should be glad to submit. Some of them, however, have been earnestly presented in previous messages, and as to them I beg leave to repeat prior recommendations.

As the law makes no provision for any report from the Department of State, a brief history of the transactions of that important department, together with other matters which it may hereafter be deemed essential to commend to the attention of the Congress, may furnish the occasion for a future communication.

GROVER CLEVELAND.

WASHINGTON, December 6, 1887.

DEMOCRATIC PLATFORM, 1888.

The Democratic party of the United States, in national convention assembled, renews the pledge of its fidelity to Democratic faith, and reaffirms the platform adopted by its representatives in the convention of 1884, and indorses the views expressed by President Cleveland in his last earnest message to Congress as the correct interpretation of that platform upon the question of tariff reduction; and also indorses the efforts of our Democratic representatives in Congress to secure a reduction of excessive taxation. Among its principles of party faith are the maintenance of the indissoluble Union of free and indestructible states, now about to enter upon its second century of unexampled progress and renown; devotion to a plan of government regulated by a written constitution strictly specifying every granted power and expressly reserving to the states or people the entire ungranted residue of power; the encouragement of a jealous popular vigilance, directed to all who have been chosen for brief terms to enact and execute the laws, and are charged with the duty of preserving peace, insuring equality, and establishing justice.

The Democratic party welcomes an exacting scrutiny of the administration of the executive power which four years ago was committed to its trust in the election of Grover Cleveland President of the United States, but it challenges the most searching inquiry concerning its fidelity and devotion to the pledges which then invited the suffrages of the people during a most critical period of our financial affairs, resulting from overtaxation, the anomalous condition of our currency, and a public debt unmatured. It has by the adoption of a wise and conservative course not only avoided disaster, but greatly promoted the prosperity of our people.

It has reversed the improvident and unwise policy of the Republican party touching the public domain, and has reclaimed from corporations and syndicates, alien and domestic, and restored to the people, nearly one hundred million acres of land, to be sacredly held as homesteads for our citizens.

While carefully guarding the interest of the principles of justice and equity, it has paid out more for pensions and bounties to the soldiers and sailors of the republic than was ever paid before during an equal period. It has adopted and consistently pursued a firm and prudent foreign policy, preserving peace with all nations while scrupulously maintaining all the rights and interests of our own government and the people at home and abroad. The exclusion from our shores of Chinese laborers has been effectually secured under the provision of a treaty, the operation of which has been postponed by the action of a Republican majority in the Senate.

In every branch and department of the government under Democratic control, the rights and the welfare of all the people have been guarded and defended; every public interest has been protected, and the equality of all our citizens before the law, without regard to race or color, has been steadfastly maintained. Upon its record, thus exhibited, and upon the pledge of a continuance to the people of the benefits of Democracy, it invokes a renewal of public trust by the reëlection of a chief magistrate who has been faithful, able, and prudent, to invoke, in addition, to that trust by the transfer also to the Democracy of the entire legislative power.

The Republican party, controlling the Senate, and resisting in both houses of Congress a reformation of unjust and unequal tax laws, which have outlasted the necessities of war and are now undermining the abundance of a long peace, deny to the people equality before the law, and the fairness and the justice which are their right. Then the cry of American labor for a better share in the rewards of industry is stifled with false pretence, enterprise is fettered and bound down to home markets, capital is discouraged with doubt, and unequal, unjust laws can neither be properly amended nor repealed.

The Democratic party will continue with all the power confided to it the struggle to reform these laws in accordance with the pledges of its last platform, indorsed at the ballot-box by the suffrages of the people. Of all the industrious freemen of our land, the immense majority, including every tiller of the soil, gain no advantage from excessive tax laws, but the price of nearly everything they buy is increased by the favoritism of an unequal system of tax legislation. All unnecessary taxation is unjust taxation.

It is repugnant to the creed of Democracy that by such taxation the cost of the necessaries of life should be unjustifiably increased to all our people. Judged by Democratic principles, the interests of the people are betrayed when, by unnecessary taxation, trusts and combinations are permitted to exist, which, while unduly enriching the few that combine, rob the body of our citizens by depriving them of the benefits of natural competition. Every Democratic rule of governmental action is violated when, through unnecessary taxation, a vast sum of money, far beyond the needs of an economical administration, is drawn from the people and the channels of trade, and accumulated as a demoralizing surplus in the national treasury. The money now lying idle in the federal treasury, resulting from superfluous taxation, amounts to more than one hundred and twenty-five millions, and the surplus collected is reaching the sum of more than sixty millions annually. Debauched by this immense temptation, the remedy of the Republican party is to meet and exhaust, by extravagant appropriations and expenses, whether constitutional or not, the accumulation of extravagant taxation. The Democratic policy is to enforce frugality in public expense, and abolish unnecessary taxation. Our established domestic industries and enterprises should not, and need not, be endangered by the reduction and correction of the burdens of taxation. On the contrary, a fair and careful revision of our tax laws, with due allowance for the difference between the wages of American and foreign labor, must promote and encourage every branch of such industries and enterprises by giving them assurances of an extended market and steady and continuous operations in the interests of American labor, which should in no event be neglected. Revision of our tax laws, contemplated by the Democratic party, should promote the advantage of such labor by cheapening the cost of necessaries of life in the home of every workingman and at the same time securing to him steady remunerative employment. Upon this question of tariff reform, so closely concerning every phase of our national life, and upon every question involved in the problem of good government, the Democratic party submits its principles and professions to the intelligent suffrages of the American people.

THE PRESIDENT'S CIVIL-SERVICE MESSAGE.

To the Congress of the United States, — Pursuant to the second section of chapter 27 of the laws of 1883, entitled "An act to regulate and improve the civil service of the United States," I herewith transmit the fourth report of the United States Civil Service Commission, covering the period between the sixteenth day of January, 1886, and the first day of July, 1887.

While this report has special reference to the operations of the commission during the period above mentioned, it contains, with its accompanying appendices, much valuable information concerning the inception of civil-service reform and its growth and progress which cannot fail to be interesting and instructive to all who desire improvement in administrative methods.

During the time covered by the report, 15,852 persons were examined for admission in the classified civil service of the government in all its branches, of whom 10,746 passed the examination, and 5,106 failed. Of those who passed the examination 2,977 were applicants for admission to the departmental service at Washington, 2,547 were examined for admission to the customs service, and 5,222 for admission to the postal service. During the same period, 547 appointments were made from the eligible lists to the departmental service, 641 to the customs service, and 3,254 to the postal service.

Concerning separations from the classified service, the report only informs us of such as have occurred among employés in the public service who had been appointed from eligible lists under civil-service rules. When these rules took effect they did not apply to the persons then in the service, comprising a full complement of employés who obtained their positions independently of the new law. The commission has no record of the separations in this numerous class, and the discrepancy apparent in the report between the number of appointments made in the respective branches of the service from the lists of the commission and the small number of separations mentioned is, to a great extent, accounted for by vacancies of which no report was made to the commission, occurring among those who held their places without examination and certification, which vacancies were filled by appointment from the eligible lists.

In the departmental service there occurred between the sixteenth day of January, 1886, and the thirtieth day of June, 1887, among the employés appointed from the eligible lists under civil-service rules, 17 removals, 36 resignations, and 5 deaths. This does not include 14 separations in the grade of special pension examiners — 4 by removal, 5 by resignation, and 5 by death.

In the classified customs and postal service, the number of separations among those who received absolute appointments under civil-service rules is given for the period between the first day of January, 1886, and the thirtieth day of June, 1887. It appears that such separations in the customs service for the time mentioned embraced 21 removals, 5 deaths, and 18 resignations, and in the postal service 256 removals, 23 deaths, and 469 resignations.

More than a year has passed since the expiration of the period covered by the report of the commission. Within the time which has thus elapsed many important changes have taken place in furtherance of a reform in our civil service. The rules and regulations governing the execution of the law upon the subject have been completely remodelled, in such manner as to render the enforcement of the statute more effective, and greatly increase its usefulness.

Among other things, the scope of the examinations prescribed for those who seek to enter the classified service has been better defined and made more practical, the number of names to be certified from the eligible lists to the appointing officers from which a selection is made has been reduced from four to three, the maximum limitation of the age of persons seeking entrance to the classified service to forty-five years has been changed, and reasonable provision has been made for the transfer of employés from one department to another in proper cases. A plan has been devised providing for the examination of applicants for promotion in the service, which, when in full operation, will eliminate all chance of favoritism in the advancement of employés, by making promotion a reward of merit and faithful discharge of duty.

Until within a few weeks there was no uniform classification of employés in the different executive departments of the government. As a result of this condition, in some of the departments positions could be obtained without civil-service examination, because they were not within the classification of such department, while in other departments an examination and certification were necessary to obtain positions of the same grade, because such positions were embraced in the classifications applicable to those departments.

The exception of laborers, watchmen, and messengers from examination and classification gave opportunity, in the absence of any rule guarding against it, for the employment, free from civil-service restrictions, of persons under these designations who were immediately detailed to do clerical work.

All this has been obviated by the application to all the departments of an extended and uniform classification embracing grades of employés not theretofore included, and by the adoption of a rule prohibiting the detail of laborers, watchmen, or messengers to clerical duty.

The path of civil-service reform has not at all times been pleasant or easy. The scope and purpose of the reform have been much misapprehended; and this has not only given rise to strong opposition, but has led to its invocation by its friends to compass objects not in the least related to it. Thus partisans of the patronage system have naturally condemned it. Those who do not understand its meaning either mistrust it or, when disappointed because in its present stage it is not applied to every real or imaginary ill, accuse those charged with its enforcement with faithlessness to civil-service reform. Its importance has frequently been underestimated; and the support of good men has thus been lost by their lack of interest in its success. Besides all these difficulties, those responsible for the administration of the government in its executive branches have been, and still are, often annoyed and irritated by the disloyalty to the service, and the insolence, of employés who remain in place as the beneficiaries and the relics and reminders of the vicious system of appointment which civil-service reform was intended to displace.

And yet these are but the incidents of an advance movement, which is radical and far-reaching. The people are, notwithstanding, to be congratulated upon the progress which has been made, and upon the firm, practical, and sensible foundation upon which this reform now rests.

With a continuation of the intelligent fidelity which has hitherto characterized the work of the commission, with a continuation and increase of the favor and liberality which have lately been evinced by the Congress in the proper equipment of the commission for its work, with a firm but conservative and reasonable support of the reform by all its friends, and with the disappearance of opposition which must inevitably follow its better understanding, the execution of the civil-service law cannot fail to ultimately answer the hopes in which it had its origin.

GROVER CLEVELAND.

EXECUTIVE MANSION, July, 23, 1888.

www.ingramcontent.com/pod-product-compliance
Lightning Source LLC
Chambersburg PA
CBHW031940230426
43672CB00010B/1998